CO-AWF-544

ALTERNATIVE WORK SCHEDULES

Part 1: Flexitime

an AMA survey report

Stanley D. Nollen
Virginia H. Martin

A DIVISION OF AMERICAN MANAGEMENT ASSOCIATIONS

AMACOM has recently published *A Flexible Approach to Working Hours*—an 11-chapter book by J. Carroll Swart based on the author's correspondence with organizations in different industries in the U.S. This in-depth treatment of the flexitime alternative work schedule includes 21 illustrated drawbacks of flexitime and some 37 illustrated advantages. The author discusses a step-by-step approach on how to set up a flexitime program and offers two 40-item questionnaires—one for managers and a second for nonmanagers—for use in evaluating a flexitime program.

Library of Congress Cataloging in Publication Data

Nollen, Stanley D
  Flexitime.

  (Their Alternative work schedules ; v. 1) (An AMA survey report)
  Bibliography: p.
  1. Hours of labor, Flexible--United States. I. Martin, Virginia Hider, joint author. II. Title.
III. Series: American Management Association.
An AMA survey report.
HD5124.N64 vol.1 [HD5109.2.U5] 331.2'572'0973s
ISBN 0-8144-3132-1 [331.2'572'0973] 78-5932

Contents

Selected Exhibits

About the Authors

Stanley D. Nollen is an assistant professor in the School of Business Administration at Georgetown University. Alternative work schedules are one of his chief research interests. He has done research on permanent part-time employment for the U.S. Department of Labor and has made presentations to a variety of groups of business people and educators. His book (with Brenda Eddy and Virginia Martin), *Part-Time Employment: The Manager's Perspective,* will be published by Praeger in their Special Studies Series in 1978. He also does research in industrial education and training and has written articles on paid educational leave of absence for workers and on lifelong learning. In the School of Business Administration, he teaches Managerial Economics and Social Responsibilities of Business. He received his M.B.A. degree in 1970 and his Ph.D. in 1974, both from the University of Chicago.

Virginia Hider Martin was one of the United States' earliest proponents of flexitime. Her study of the experience of public and private sector organizations with flexible working hours, *Hours of Work When Workers Can Choose,* was published in 1975. An independent organizational development consultant in Alexandria, Virginia, and teacher of a short course on flexitime implementation, she was a founder of the National Council for Alternative Work Patterns and chaired the program committee for the first National Conference on Alternative Work Schedules. She is a member of the American Society for Training and Development and the Industrial Relations Research Association, and co-author with Stanley Nollen and Brenda Eddy of a book on part-time employment that is to be published by Praeger in 1978.

Introduction

Interest in alternative work schedules is high and rising—especially among management and labor groups. In addition, some professional associations and research institutes are calling for more study and development of such schedules. A number of national and regional conferences on the topic have been held for business, labor, government, and academic people in the last two years. These schedules are being supported by several advocacy groups—including those representing the interests of women, retirees, the handicapped, and environmentalists. Media attention is growing, including that of the business press. Several pieces of legislation on alternative work schedules are pending in the U.S. Congress, and some states have already enacted such legislation. (See Appendix B.) And employers themselves, in both private and public sectors, have begun experiments with alternative work schedules; many such schedules are currently in use.

What Are Alternative Work Schedules?

The term *alternative work schedules* encompasses all variations of the standard work schedule: that is, a workday from 8:00 or 9:00 a.m. to 5:00 p.m., for seven or eight hours a day, five days a week. Chief among such systems are:

- *Flexible Working Hours (Flexitime).* Employees may vary their starting and stopping times within limits, but work the contracted number of hours in a specified time period (day, week, or month).
- *The Compressed Workweek.* The usual number of weekly full-time hours is compressed into fewer than five days.
- *Permanent Part-Time Employment.* Regular, voluntary employment (not temporary or casual) carried out during working hours distinctly shorter than normal.

Another major alternative work pattern is staggered hours, in which some employees are scheduled to arrive and depart earlier (7:30 a.m. to 4:30 p.m., for example) than others (who may, for example, arrive at 8:30 a.m. and leave at 5:30 p.m.). Sometimes this system is instituted on a communitywide basis as a traffic relief measure. Employers are asked to adopt starting times outside the peak commuting period. Such a program sponsored by the Port Authority of New York and New Jersey has succeeded in alleviating rush hour congestion in midtown and lower Manhattan (Port Authority, 1977). In other cases, staggered starting times have been established for different groups of workers within one firm. If the staggered hours are chosen by employees, rather than assigned by management, this system is considered a restricted form of flexitime.

The task system is another alternative work schedule—one simply assigns a task or specified quantity of work to be completed within a given time period. In practice, a day's work is usually assigned and employees are free to leave when it is finished. This system, also known as earned time, has been instituted for production workers at Harman International Industries' Bolivar, Tennessee, automobile mirror plant as part of a joint labor-management project to improve the quality of working life. (See the testimony of Sidney Harman in U.S. Congress, Senate, 1976.) It is also used for sanitation workers (trash collectors) in many cities. Few other examples of this system exist. Neither this task system nor the staggered hours system is reported on in this study.

In the alternative work schedules survey, we addressed only the three major schedules: flexitime, the compressed workweek, and permanent part-time employment. This report, which is Part 1 of the overall report, gives and discusses only the results pertaining to *flexitime*. Parts 2 and 3, to be published in a later report, will give and discuss the results pertaining to the compressed workweek and permanent part-time employment.

Flexitime is a relatively new development in industrial relations—a relatively new idea in the employment policies of organizations. Beginning in Germany in 1967, it spread rapidly throughout Europe but received little attention in the U.S. until 1972. Basically a strategy for developing human resources, flexitime certainly serves the best interests of workers. But its appeal lies in the fact that it offers benefits to employers as well as to workers, and that the public interest is also likely to be served.

The State of Current Knowledge

How widely is flexitime being used? Who is using it? What experiences do employers have with it? What good results does it actually yield to the organization? What problems does it bring? How does management respond? Before we report on the results revealed in this study, a look at what we already know is in order.

Guesses about the number of workers on flexitime have been running about 1 percent. The only previous survey evidence is that 3 percent of 212 responding firms from a sample of 500 members of the American Society for Personnel Administration were using flexitime in 1974. Another 4 percent were using employee-chosen staggered hours, which is equivalent to a restricted version of flexitime (Martin, 1975). These estimates may be high because of the nature of the sample, its small size, and response bias. It is widely believed, however, that flexitime is growing. It has also been thought—without documentation—that flexitime is more suitable for office jobs and less suitable for factory jobs, especially with shift work. But successful usage in shift operations has been reported (Young, 1976; Hopp and Sommerstad, 1975).

A variety of benefits have been claimed for flexitime, both for employers and for workers. Correspondingly, a number of disadvantages have been suggested. Some of these supposedly good points and bad points have been evaluated in case studies of organizations (see, for example, Jaffe, Friedman, and Rogers, forthcoming; Golembiewski, Hilles, and Kagno, 1974; Hopp and Sommerstad, 1975; Schein, 1977; White, forthcoming; U.S. Geological Survey, 1975, and Hedges, 1977 for an overview and summary), and a few surveys have been made (Martin, 1975; Weinstein, 1975). From these studies, and from theoretical expectations, a number of statements about the advantages and disadvantages of flexitime can be tentatively offered.

In general, flexitime is expected to increase employee morale and job satisfaction—which may in turn reduce turnover, absenteeism, and tardiness and make recruiting easier. Productivity may also be improved. On the negative side, flexitime appears to raise new management difficulties and require additional supervisory inputs. It may cause some scheduling problems and make communication more difficult. As we shall see later, however, the potential scheduling and communication problems may be overrated, and apparently they can be overcome.

Previous studies also indicate that when employees can choose their work hours, not only are their morale and job satisfaction likely to go up, but also their commuting problems can be eased and they can better integrate home and family life with work life. From the employer's standpoint, tardiness is virtually eliminated by definition under flexitime systems in which workers can vary their daily starting and stopping times. Since workers usually prefer flexitime over a standard 9:00 to 5:00 schedule, turnover is often reduced and recruiting made easier. Employers report that productivity often increases—perhaps because of increased job satisfaction, or because workers will naturally select hours of work that are best for them (both "morning" people and "night" people can be accommodated), or because less "settling in" time is wasted since neighboring work colleagues are likely to be either already at work or not yet present. People are also more likely to finish a task before going home, instead of laying it down half complete at the end of the day—or not beginning it at all. In addition, capital equipment, space, and facilities might be more efficiently used. Customer service can also be extended, since the office or plant will ordinarily be staffed both earlier and later in the day under flexitime. However, previous studies also report that none of these frequent advantages is invariably experienced; none can be routinely expected.

On the negative side, previous research reports that flexitime often increases the difficulty of the manager's job, most likely because varying arrival and departure times for employees create problems in scheduling work tasks and covering essential functions—especially in small organizations. Similarly, both internal and external communication may take longer if some workers are not present during early or late hours. But previous studies find less empirical evidence of communication problems than is usually suspected. Because flexitime often means that offices or plants are open longer each day, fears of increased utilities costs and support services costs (stemming from security and the cafeteria, for example) have been expressed. However, not much evidence has been found to verify these fears.

Research Objectives and Methods

There are several questions about the use of flexitime for which there are now no satisfactory answers. The objective of this study is to provide answers to these questions. In general, these key questions are:

1. How extensively is flexitime used? How many employers have adopted it? Have any discontinued it? How many workers are on it?
2. Which of the several flexitime models are most common? How much flexibility is there? Are core times usual?
3. What kinds of jobs and work settings are suited to the use of flexitime? Who are the users and the non-users? Does flexitime fit some industries and operating schedules better than others? Is it more common in large or in small firms?

4. How does flexitime affect the whole range of possible business results—from productivity to public relations, from employee morale to management problems, from direct labor costs to overhead costs? Are there hard data to document these results?
5. What explains the good results and the bad results of flexitime usage? What characteristics of organizations and their managements are likely to improve the results? Which of the various flexitime models gives the best results?
6. How do the business results of flexitime usage change with longer experience? Do good results hold up—or do they spring from a kind of Hawthorne effect and thus die off quickly? Do negative aspects persist or can they be overcome with more experience?
7. How is flexitime implemented? What management steps are involved? What changes are made elsewhere in the organization? What problems are encountered? How are they solved?
8. What role do labor unions play in the use of flexitime? Under what conditions do they assist in or oppose its implementation? How many workers on flexitime are union members?

Previous surveys by Martin (1975) and Weinstein (1975) form the empirical basis for this research, but they are limited by the small number of users surveyed (n=59 in Martin's research—and n=35 in Weinstein's).

By contrast, the larger number of flexitime users uncovered in this study (196) permits more reliable answers, better projections, and a more precise analysis of reasons for certain results. The existence of the previous surveys permits some comparisons to be made of employers' experiences with flexitime over a period of time—thus providing a longer-run view of results and problems than employers contemplating flexitime implementation might expect.

The research basis for this report is 805 returned mail questionnaires (28 percent) from a survey of 2,889 organizations conducted in June and July 1977 on alternative work schedules—

flexitime, the compressed workweek, and permanent part-time employment. Two populations were sampled: (1) 2,091 organizations in which a senior manager (president, vice-president for human resources, or personnel director, for example) was a customer of the American Management Associations in 1975-77, by virtue of either seminar attendance or publication purchase and (2) 798 suspected users of one or more alternative work schedules. The latter sample was necessary to provide a large enough number of users from which to learn experiences. A substantial number of responses was secured from each of several major industry groups and size-of-firm groups. A variety of operating schedules and work technologies are represented, and organizations with both heavy and light union membership and female employment are in the sample.

An additional 100 mini-interviews with non-respondents among the customer list were conducted by telephone to determine the direction and magnitude of response bias that might have resulted. These results were used to adjust key projections of flexitime usage and its major effects on business. (See Appendix A.) The following analysis of flexitime usage focuses primarily on the experiences of 196 users uncovered in the mailed returns—with some comparisons with non-users.

1
Highlights and Conclusions

Flexible working hours, or flexitime, is a new and growing alternative work schedule. Under flexitime, employees may vary their starting and stopping times within limits while they work the contracted number of hours in a specified time period. They may, for example, come to work anytime between 7:00 and 9:30 a.m. and leave anytime between 4:00 and 6:30 p.m. according to their choice, as long as they work eight hours a day—40 hours a week. (This schedule includes one unpaid hour for lunch.)

For workers, the fundamental feature of flexible working hours is a new freedom of choice and autonomy. This flexibility enhances the quality and dignity of working life by offering them more control over their working time and the ability to accommodate personal and family life needs as well as work needs. Flexitime treats workers as responsible adults and may increase job satisfaction. As a respondent in a large governmental agency in the Northeast said, "Employees are provided with the opportunity to mesh their personal schedules with their work schedules and thereby function in a more mature responsible manner." It removes the emphasis from hours worked to work performed. And, though this is yet largely unrealized, it may also facilitate lifelong learning since the new time-management possibilities involved permit adult workers to take advantage of educational opportunities.

Flexitime also offers benefits to employers. There is both the potentially higher productivity to be gained from more satisfied and more highly motivated workers and the prospect of using the flexible hours feature of jobs to attract people with high-level capabilities. In addition, it poses new flexibility for employers as well as workers. It expands the range of options for solving scheduling problems and meeting customer service needs. The fact that flexitime implementation costs very little in visible dollars and cents also appeals to employers. However, it does present a management challenge and, at least initially, requires new management thinking and additional management inputs.

Two major sets of social benefits may flow from the use of flexitime among organizations. First, a variety of public services and facilities can be provided more efficiently—with fewer, and less steep, peaks and valleys. Chief among these are more evenly distributed commuting traffic flows, demands for public transportation (with potentially reduced energy consumption), and use of recreational facilities. Second, employment opportunities for several groups of people are improved—particularly women, men who wish a more balanced work and home life, the handicapped, and the aging.

How Much Flexitime Is There?
Projections made from this survey indicate that for the U.S. in 1977

- 12.8 percent of all nongovernment organizations with 50 or more employees used flexitime.

5

- 5.8 percent of all employees were on flexitime.
- Between 2.5 and 3.5 million employees were on flexitime, not counting self-employed people and many professionals, managers, and salespeople who have long set their own hours without calling their schedules flexitime.

Flexitime use has increased rapidly, perhaps doubling from 1974 to 1977. And since nine percent of all organizations are currently planning or evaluating its use, it is likely to continue its rapid gains.

Flexitime is somewhat more popular in some industries than others. Nationwide projections indicate the following usage pattern among selected industries:
- 10.3 percent in manufacturing
- 17.1 percent in transportation, communication, and utilities
- 14.4 percent in wholesale and retail trade
- 19.3 percent in finance and insurance
- 14.4 percent in service industries

Flexitime Models

Although various models of flexitime are being used, most permit daily variation in starting and stopping times—with a core period when all workers must be present. Fewer than half the flexitime systems in use permit more than eight hours to be worked in a day, and very few permit employees to borrow or carry hours over from one week or pay period to the next.

Timekeeping under flexitime is most frequently based on the honor system for exempt employees and on manual records or time clocks for non-exempt employees. A large majority of employees choose to come to work earlier under flexitime than they were required to do previously.

Where is Flexitime Not Used?

Among organizations using flexitime, nearly half make it available to all work units. Overall, 45 percent of all employees in user organizations are on flexitime.

The use of flexitime in some work activities, however, is reported to be unfeasible by a fifth to a third of all experienced users. These activities are (1) shift work and assembly lines or other machine-paced work, (2) work where continuous coverage is needed, (3) work in small organizations or where there are few workers, and (4) jobs where extensive communication and interfacing is needed.

Experiences of Flexitime Users

Flexitime has several important effects on the organizations that use it. Good effects reported (from all major industries) indicate that it:
- Raises employee morale—almost always.
- Reduces tardiness—in 84 percent of the cases.
- Eases employee commuting—more than three-quarters of the time.
- Reduces absenteeism—nearly three-quarters of the time.
- Makes recruiting easier—in 65 percent of the cases.
- Reduces turnover—more than half the time.
- Increases productivity—for almost half the users.

But flexitime also has a few negative effects that pose new challenges to management. For example, it:
- Increases the difficulty of the management job—for half the users.
- Worsens internal communication—in 38 percent of the cases.

Other management aspects of flexitime reflect mixed results; they are advantages about as often as they are problems, depending on the user. For example:
- Coverage of work situations is better under flexitime for 30 percent of the users, but worse for 38 percent of them.
- Employee scheduling is better for 27 percent of the users but worse for 38 percent of them.

Most business costs are not affected by flexitime. For example, most users believe that utilities and support services costs remain the same, although few have actual measurements. Relationships with customers likewise are usually not affected, one way or the other.

Several of the chief advantages and problems reported by flexitime users are data-based in a substantial number of cases. For example, as many as two-thirds of the absenteeism reports are data-based, while 40 percent of the users measure the difficulty of the management job. But effects on direct costs, including utilities costs and unit labor costs, are usually not measured, hence assessments reflect only employers' educated guesses.

Does Flexitime Work Better in Some Work Settings Than in Others?

In general, flexitime experiences are not much different for organizations in one industry, work technology, or group size than another. Manufacturing firms, organizations with mass-production work technologies, and small firms (all presumably difficult cases for flexitime) do not have a worse experience with flexitime overall than other users. Of course, this does not mean that flexitime can be used anywhere—since specific work settings could not be compared in this survey, and many flexitime employees in manufacturing or mass-production firms may work in offices rather than in production or on assembly lines.

What Do Non-Users Think?

Employers who do not use flexitime have about the same expectations of its good effects on the organization as users actually experience. But they foresee more problems, particularly in terms of communication, management aspects, and some costs. These more negative views arise not from characteristics of non-users (such as their industry) that differ from those of users; rather, it appears that non-users could obtain better results from flexitime than they realize. The spread of flexitime, then, does not seem to be constrained by a lack of opportunities among current non-users.

Long-Term Effects of Flexitime

Do the good effects of flexitime last? Do they endure after flexitime has been used several years and becomes routine? The answer is *yes,* without exception. Just as many long-term flexitime users report improved employee relations and job performance as do short-term users. A sub-sample of flexitime users in this 1977 survey reported about the same experiences that they did in 1974 in a longitudinal comparison.

The occasional problems raised by flexitime continue to require attention in the long run. Coverage, scheduling, and communication problems continue to occur a quarter to a third of the time among long-term users of flexitime. This situation may result from a tendency among long-term users to reintroduce change by increasing the flexibility of their flexitime systems.

Implementation of Flexitime

A majority of the organizations that use flexitime took several implementation steps before adopting it. Following are the steps they most frequently took.

Planning phase:
- Held meetings with managers and supervisors—85 percent.
- Held meetings with employees—67 percent.
- Reviewed federal and state labor laws—61 percent.
- Discussed plan with other organizations—61 percent.
- Sent an organization member to a seminar or conference—54 percent.

Adoption phase
- Instituted first on trial basis—86 percent.
- Changed operating schedules (for example, held offices open to employees or public for longer hours or rearranged shifts)—70 percent.

Other implementation steps that are feasible—but were taken less than half the time—are (1) appointing an internal project director and (2) providing for an audit of the results. Outside consultants were seldom engaged; work was seldom restructured.

Does Implementation Affect Outcomes?

Chances of success in using flexitime can be increased by alleviating some of the problems involved. Experience has shown that scheduling and communication are less likely to be problems for users who take some or all of the following implementation steps:

- Appoint an internal project director.
- Hold meetings with managers or supervisors.
- Hold meetings with employees.
- Institute flexitime on a trial basis at first.

The appointment of an internal flexitime project director also alleviated the chief problem flexitime poses—that of making management's job more difficult. Since fewer than half the user organizations took this step, it becomes a priority change for future flexitime implementers.

Flexitime Problems and Solutions

Well over half the problems encountered by flexitime users are management or supervision problems, including scheduling and coverage problems. But these problems were solved most frequently by the employees themselves—who, for example, agreed to meet minimum staffing requirements or rotate their schedules and cover for each other. First-line supervisors were educated in the nature of their role—from one of negative control to one of positive planning. Sometimes, too, an attitude change was involved —with the new attitude summed up by the expression, "If you treat people as adults, they act as adults." Occasionally, modifications of the flexitime system were required to suit individual aspects of the work or the employees involved.

Flexitime Failures: How Often and Why

Like any management innovation, flexitime does not always succeed. But its failure rate is low. There were 13 continuing successful uses of flexitime for every failure. Among those who discontinued flexitime, over half did so before a year of use was up.

Flexitime discontinuers do not differ obviously in industry, size, or other characteristics from the organizations that continue flexitime use. Reasons given for dropping flexitime were varied—ranging from an inability to provide adequate supervision, which created scheduling and coverage problems, to difficulties with timekeeping.

2

Extent and Patterns of Flexitime Usage

Flexible working hours, or flexitime, is the newest of the alternative schedules to gain substantial usage among organizations in the U.S. (See Exhibit 1 for a description of the survey sample

Exhibit 1. The sample of 196 flexitime users: Industry, sector, and size.

Category	Percent of All Users
Industry	
Manufacturing	36
Transportation, communications, and utilities	9
Wholesale and retail trade	5
Finance, insurance, real estate	25
Services	9
Government	16
Sector	
Private	81
profit	74
nonprofit	7
Public	19
Number of Employees	
fewer than 100	7
100 to 499	21
500 to 1000	16
more than 1000	56
Annual Sales or Budget	
under $25 million	27
$25 to $99 million	19
$100 to $999 million	32
over $1 billion	22

of flexitime users in terms of industry, sector, size, and work technology of respondents.) It encompasses a variety of arrangements that give employees some choice in their work schedule. Flexitime systems differ in the degree of flexibility employees have in determining both (1) their starting and stopping times and (2) their total hours worked in a day or other time period.

The most restricted form of flexitime permits employees to choose one schedule and then requires them to follow that schedule regularly. The most liberal flexitime model permits employees to choose any schedule they wish, including daily variations in starting and stopping times and in hours worked, with provisions for carrying over hours or borrowing hours from one pay period to the next.

Core time is a feature of some flexitime systems. It refers to a period during the workday when all employees must be present. There may be one core time (9:00 a.m. to 4:00 p.m, for example) with a fixed lunch period, or there may be two core times—one in the morning (9:00 to 11:30 a.m., for example) and one in the afternoon (1:30 to 4:00 p.m., for example)—in which case employees also have flexibility in their lunch periods. (See Exhibit 2.)

How Widely Is Flexitime Used?

Results from this survey research indicate that the use of flexitime is quite high indeed and is

Exhibit 2. Flexitime schedules contrasted with traditional fixed schedule.

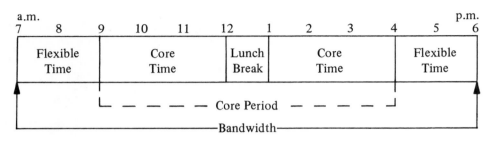

Traditional Fixed 8-hour Day

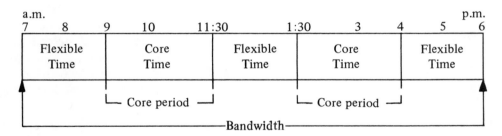

Flexible Day with Single Core Period

Flexible Day with Double Core Period

increasing rapidly. Nationwide, an estimated 12.8 percent of all private sector organizations use flexitime (the projection refers to nongovernment organizations with 50 or more employees). This estimate is based on a usage rate of 14.3 percent among the 495 respondents to a mail questionnaire sent to 2,091 customers of the American Management Associations (see Exhibit 3), adjusted for response bias and for differences in the industries of these respondents as compared with U.S. figures.* This 1977 usage rate exceeds the estimated 1974 usage rate of 7 percent (unadjusted for response bias or representa-

tiveness) obtained by Virginia Martin from a smaller sample.

An additional 9 percent of all employers nationwide are estimated to be currently planning or evaluating the use of flexitime. (Six percent of the sample stated they were planning or evaluating flexitime use, and this figure rises to 9 percent when adjusted for response bias and unrepresentativeness.) This means that if as few as half of those now planning or evaluating flexitime implement it in the next year, the usage rate will rise to 17.3 percent in 1978.

The number of employees currently on flexitime is roughly estimated to be 5.8 percent nationwide—based on an estimate that organizations using flexitime include, on the average, about 45 percent of their workforce in the flexitime

*Response bias is not large. Among 100 random telephone callback interviews with nonrespondents, 11 percent were flexitime users. See Appendix A for more detail on response bias, for the adjustments made to correct for it, for the industrial distribution of respondents, and for other sources of error.

Exhibit 3. Estimated extent of flexitime usage in the U.S., 1977.

Measure of Usage	Sample[a] (percent)	U.S. Projection[b] (percent)
Number of organizations currently using flexitime	14.3	12.8
Number of employees on flexitime[c]	6.4	5.8
Number of organizations currently planning or evaluating use of flexitime	6.5	9.0
Predicted number of organizations using flexitime in 1978[d]	17.5	17.3
Predicted number of employees on flexitime in 1978	7.9	7.8

Notes:

[a]Sample size = 495.

[b]U.S. projections obtained from data on usage rates by industry, on the U.S. distribution of firms by industry, and on the degree of response bias in the sample (see Appendix A).

[c]Based on survey data that, on the average, organizations using flexitime include 45 percent of their workforce in the system.

[d]Assuming half of those employers currently planning or evaluating flexitime usage implement it in the next year.

system. This figure indicates that the use of flexitime is much more widespread than previously thought, since many guesses have been around 1 percent. The percentage in 1978 is predicted to be 7.8 percent. (These estimates assume that large firms and small firms do not differ in the proportion of their workforce on flexitime.) An estimate of the number of people working flexible schedules nationwide falls between 2.5 and 3.5 million, based on this survey but using many assumptions in addition (see Appendix A). This figure does not include the several million self-employed people and those professionals, managers, and salespeople who have long set their own schedules without calling this procedure flexitime.

Flexitime Models

Among the 196 current users of flexitime in this study, the most frequent flexitime models permit daily variation in starting and stopping times (79 percent), do not permit more than the standard eight hours a day to be worked (52 percent)—see Appendix B for a discussion of constraints on flexitime imposed by wage and hour law—and do have core time (88 percent). Among employers who permit daily variation in starting and stopping times, about half require advance notice of schedule changes from workers. In only a handful of cases are employees able to carry over hours or borrow hours from one week or pay period to the next. As Exhibit 4 shows, almost all employers make use of core time, with the use of a single core time (involving a fixed lunch period) outnumbering the use of two core times (a morning core and an afternoon core, with a flexible lunch period).

How much do employees use the flexibility that flexitime gives them? In what way do they

Exhibit 4. Flexitime models in use in the U.S., 1977 (n = 195).

Flexitime Model	Percent of All Users
Flexibility in arrival and departure time	
Employees may vary their schedules daily	79
with advance notice	41
without advance notice	38
Employees must choose one schedule and follow it regularly	21
Flexibility in hours worked	
Employees may not work more than 8 hours in any one day unless overtime is authorized	52
Employees may work more than 8 hours per day but not more than 40 hours per week unless overtime is authorized	28
Employees may carry over or borrow hours from one week or pay period to the next	8
Other and no answer	12
Core time	
Have core time	88
Single core time with fixed lunch period	49
Two core times, morning and afternoon, with flexible lunch period	39
No core time	12

Exhibit 5. Changes in work schedules after flexitime implementation (n = 196).

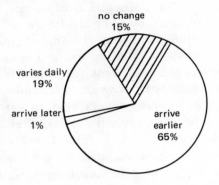

no change
15%

varies daily
19%

arrive later
1%

arrive earlier
65%

change their schedules? As Exhibit 5 shows, an overwhelming majority—85 percent—do choose a different personal schedule under flexitime than before, and almost all of them come to work earlier rather than later. But a relatively small number of employees vary their starting and stopping times from one day to the next, even when they are permitted to do so (only 25 percent of those who have this option make use of it).

Patterns of Flexitime Usage

The overall nationwide usage of flexitime by 12.8 percent of all organizations conceals some differences between organizations that use it frequently and those that use it less frequently—differences tied to organizational characteristics. Flexitime usage patterns are better understood by looking at (1) the usage rate in different industries, sectors, and firm sizes, and (2) comparisons between flexitime users and non-users in their levels of female employment, union membership, work technology, and use of other alternative work schedules.

● *Industry and sector.* The use of flexitime is somewhat more popular in some industries than others, but the differences in usage rates are not large (see Exhibit 6). The category with the largest number of organizations using flexitime is the finance/insurance/real estate category, with a usage rate of 19.3 percent, while the industry least likely to use flexitime is manufacturing, where 10.3 percent of all organizations are users (these figures are nationwide projections made

after taking response bias into account). The extent of flexitime usage in the private sector appears to be little different from its usage in the public sector, although there were too few responses from using and non-using public sector enterprises (n=16) to allow valid comparisons.

● *Size of firm.* The use of flexitime may vary somewhat by size of firm, but the differences are modest and the trend is not uniform. Exhibit 6 shows that in the largest firms (1,000 or more employees), for example, 13.5 percent use flexitime, while in the smallest firms (100 to 499 employees), 8.8 percent use it. But medium-sized firms (500 to 999 employees) have the greatest use, 18.1 percent.

● *Female employment.* Flexitime users are somewhat more likely to have a high proportion of women employees than are non-users: 38 percent of the users have a workforce in which over half the employees are female, compared

Exhibit 6. Flexitime usage rate by industry, sector, and size of firm in the U.S., 1977

Item	Percent of Organizations Using
Industry	
manufacturing	10.3
transportation, communications, utilities	17.1
wholesale, retail trade	14.4
finance, insurance, real estate	19.3
services	14.4
all industries	12.8
Sector	
private	12.9
profit	13.0
nonprofit	9.7
public	17.6
all sectors	12.8
Size of Firm (number of employees)	
50 to 1,000	12.5
50 to 499	8.6
500 to 1,000	17.1
>1,000	13.1
all sizes (≥ 50 employees)	12.8

Note: Percentages are based on responses from 495 organizations that are customers of the American Management Associations. The figures are adjusted for response bias and are intended to be nationwide projections (see Appendix A).

Exhibit 7. Differences between 196 flexitime users and 374 non-users in the U.S., 1977.

	Users (percent)	Non-Users (percent)
Female Employment		
less than 25 percent	17	36
25 to 50 percent	45	37
more than 50 percent	38	28
Labor Union Membership		
none	58	46
1 to 24 percent	18	14
25 to 75 percent	18	33
more than 75 percent	5	6
Work Technology		
office work	95	84
factory work	52	78
services produced	50	36
goods produced	33	53
unit production; single, nonstandardized items	14	17
mass production; assembly line	15	27
each worker's tasks require presence of other workers	23	35
one worker's output is another worker's input	44	42
can use buffer inventories for in-process items	19	22
produce for immediate delivery	19	28
heavy internal communication required	65	46
communication required across time zones	59	37
heavy contact with outside suppliers or customers	59	51

with 28 percent of the non-users where this is the case. (See Exhibit 7.)

• *Union membership.* Flexitime users are less likely than non-users to have substantial union representation: As Exhibit 7 shows, only 23 percent of users had as much as a quarter of their workforce represented by unions, compared with 39 percent of non-users where this was the case. Over half of the users had no union membership at all. Of course, the differences between flexitime users and non-users—both in the level of female employment and in labor union membership—may be traceable to the relatively low rate of flexitime usage by firms in the manufacturing industry, which constituted a large share of the sample.

• *Work technology.* Work technology refers to (1) the nature of a job and what is required to do it (for example, the production processes, communication requirements, and co-worker relationships involved) and (2) external demands made on the work unit (scheduling requirements, for example, or relationships with customers or suppliers). There are many different dimensions along which to describe work technology and many different aspects that could be measured. Here, only those aspects expected to have an effect on flexitime usage were included (based on previous indications from business people).

Compared with non-users, organizations that use flexitime are more likely to be offices than factories, and more likely to be predominantly services producers than goods producers.

A closer look at work technology confirms some previous beliefs about its relationship to flexitime usage but does not confirm others. For example, flexitime is frequently considered to be incompatible with mass production technologies and assembly lines because the unpredictable or variable arrival and departure times of flexitime employees would prevent assembly-line work stations from being staffed continuously, without interruption. And, indeed, mass-production and assembly lines are characteristic of only 15 percent of all flexitime users—less than the 27 percent frequency among non-users. Similarly, there are relatively few instances of flexitime usage in organizations where each worker's tasks require the presence of other workers—a circumstance required in assembly-line production.

Note, however, that flexitime is not rigidly incompatible with mass-production technology—it is only less common than in other technologies. Flexitime *is* occasionally used together with mass production, and new management strategies for implementing flexitime in mass-production technologies are being developed.

Another type of work technology that has been considered unsuitable for flexitime is work in which one worker's output is another worker's input (in nonline product assembly, for example,

Exhibit 8. Frequency with which flexitime users and non-users use other alternative work schedules.

Item	Flexitime Users (n=194) percent	Flexitime Non-Users (n=370) percent
Flexitime Use with the Compressed Workweek:		
Use compressed workweek	25	15
Have considered or are planning use of compressed workweek	21	10
Discontinued compressed workweek	8	7
Do not use compressed workweek	46	68
Flexitime Use with Permanent Part-Time Employment		
Use permanent part-time employment	72	54
Have considered or are planning use of permanent part-time employment	11	5
Discontinued permanent part-time employment	0	1
Do not use permanent part-time employment	17	40

Note: Usage percentages may be used for comparisons, but are not valid absolute estimates of usage.

or in office operations where mail is sorted, delivered, read, and relayed to various departments —accounting, shipping, and so forth). Where some workers do not have their output ready for other workers (perhaps because their schedules do not coincide), then flexitime might be unsatisfactory unless buffer inventories are maintained. However, this survey indicates that fully as many users as non-users of flexitime—nearly half—have this work technology in their organization; yet few users maintain buffer inventories. Thus a work technology in which one worker's output is another worker's input need not *in principle* deter the implementation of flexitime. Of course, some of these firms may have their flexitime employees working at jobs outside this technology, so they are not affected by it.

Another widely expressed concern about flexitime is that it might not be suitable in work technologies requiring extensive communication— either internally at the work site or across time zones to other organizations. In addition, requirements for frequent contact with outside suppliers or customers has been thought a deterrent to flexitime. All of these concerns stem from the possibility that some employees might not be at work by 9:00 a.m. or until 5:00 p.m.—

thus making communication difficult. But, in fact, the evidence is that these communication-related work technologies are found among flexitime users *more* frequently than among non-users. This result suggests that a potential advantage of flexitime in these technologies—more total hours in the day during which communication can take place or customers' needs can be met—outweighs the potential disadvantages. In order to have staff available at all hours, workers may be crosstrained and minimum coverage requirements set for each department at various times of day. Thus an organization with a wide band of flexible hours overall might have a narrower band for some units—or workers might be permitted maximum flexibility if they agreed to take turns meeting minimum coverage needs.

• *Other alternative work schedules.* Flexitime users are more likely to use other alternative work schedules than are non-users. Both compressed workweeks and permanent part-time employment are found more often in the organizations that use flexitime than in those that don't. Flexitime users are also more likely to have considered or to be currently planning the use of compressed workweeks and permanent part-time employment (see Exhibit 8). Thus in-

Exhibit 9. Where flexitime is and is not used.

	Percent of 196 Users
Flexitime is used:	
in all units in the organization (whole company, division, or branch)	42
in all units except those on shifts, where crews are used, or on assembly lines	7
in certain units (e.g., personnel department, systems department, office administration)	44
other	7
for exempt employees only	3
for non-exempt employees only	11
for both exempt and non-exempt employees	86
by less than 10 percent of the workers	22
by 10 to 24 percent	21
by 25 to 49 percent	13
by 50 to 75 percent	11
by more than 75 percent of the workers	33

	Percent of 180 Responses
Flexitime is not feasible:	
for shift work, assembly lines, machine-paced work	30
where continuous coverage is needed (e.g., receptionist, retail sales floor, receiving room, mail room, nursing unit, bus driving, security, or in small organizations or where there are few workers)	28
where extensive communication, coordination, or interfacing is needed within the company or with customers or the public	21
in service and support functions that are needed often and immediately (e.g., secretaries)	7
in other activities (e.g., administration, computer operations) where close supervision is required	14

stead of being substitutes for each other, alternative work schedules appear to complement each other.

Where is Flexitime Used in the Organization? Where Is It Not Feasible?

When flexitime is used in an organization, it tends to be quite widespread—that is, available to a large number of workers rather than restricted to only a few work units or jobs (see Exhibit 9). In 42 percent of user organizations (here, the work *organization* refers to the whole company in 70 percent of the cases, and to the head-

quarters location or to a division or branch in 20 percent of the cases), flexitime is used in all work units. In another 7 percent of the organizations, flexitime is used in all units except those whose work technologies are considered incompatible—on shifts, for example, or where crews are used, or on assembly lines (and, of course, where workers already set their own hours, as do some salespeople and some managers). In the balance of the organizations, flexitime is used only in certain individual work units.

In 44 percent of organizations using flexitime, over half of the workers are on the system. Relatively few organizations restrict flexitime to a small group of employees. Correspondingly, flexitime is available to both exempt and non-exempt employees in most organizations (86 percent).

Where is flexitime not used? For what kinds of work activities is it not feasible? There is no consensus among flexitime users on where it would not work; there is no single category of work activity that as many as a third of all users report to be unfeasible. Instead, there are three different kinds of work activities that are sometimes mentioned: (1) shift work, assembly lines, and machine-paced work (30 percent); (2) work where continuous coverage is needed—involving, for example, receptionists, switchboard operators, and security personnel or in small organizations or where there are few workers (28 percent); and

(3) jobs where extensive communication and interfacing is needed, whether inside or outside the company (21 percent).

Flexitime is also less likely to be used in departments where employees are represented by unions. Among nine out of ten users, fewer than 25 percent of the flexitime employees were union members. By contrast, union membership was more common in the *overall* workforce of users—about six out of ten users had as little as 25 percent union membership. Only seven percent of the organizations that use flexitime report that more than half of their employees are union members. Thus unionized companies are both less likely to use flexitime at all, and they are less likely to include union members even if they do use flexitime.

3
Effects of Flexitime on the Organization

Flexitime may have several important effects on the organizations that use it—effects on workers, on job performance, on management practices, on a variety of costs, and even on people outside the organizations. What are these effects? Which are good and which are bad? Are these effects favorable overall?

Experiences of Flexitime Users

According to the experiences of 196 user organizations, flexitime has almost universally good effects on workers and strongly positive effects on job performance (but with some communication problems). It poses challenges to management, but usually has little effect on costs.*

*As we shall subsequently document, some of the flexitime experiences differ by industry. Although the sample of flexitime users in this study does not conform to the national distribution of firms by industry, the overall experiences reported are not distorted. This is because a disproportionately large number of responses were received from both industries usually reporting favorable experiences and those usually reporting unfavorable experiences.

In addition, bias in reported experiences because of nonresponse is negligible. The frequency of good and bad experiences in three key areas (employee morale, productivity, and coverage) were determined from 50 telephone interviews with randomly selected nonrespondents to the mail questionnaire who were flexitime users. After minor adjustments were made for differences in the industrial distribution of the two groups (mail questionnaire respondents versus telephoned nonrespondents), there was not a statistically significant difference between them in their experiences except for coverage. In that case, response bias was negative—that is, fewer nonrespondents reported worse coverage caused by flexitime than did respondents. Thus the incidence of bad experiences with coverage is, if anything, overestimated in this report.

Effects on workers. Above all else, flexitime is good for workers. As a respondent from a medium-size insurance company in the Mid-Atlantic region said, "One's job does not have to determine the structure of one's life." Another respondent noted equality of treatment as an advantage of flexitime—that is, that non-exempt and exempt workers are treated as equals in regard to working hours. Flexitime improved employee morale in 97 percent of the organizations using it, and it aided employee commuting in 77 percent of them (see Exhibit 10). Thus the increased freedom of choice, autonomy, and also responsibility that flexitime provides pay off in the form of more satisfied workers.

Effects on job performance. By any common measure, job performance is likely to improve under flexitime; it seldom worsens. Of the user organizations, 48 percent reported increased productivity after the introduction of flexitime, and 53 percent reported a reduction in turnover. Absenteeism was even more frequently reduced—in 73 percent of the organizations—and tardiness was reduced in most cases (84 percent), as would be expected in a system whose nature virtually eliminates it. According to a respondent from a medium-size manufacturing company in the Southeast, flexitime "allows employees to take care of personal affairs without resorting to 'sick' leave." Thus while flexitime is good for workers, it also yields a dividend to employers.

Exhibit 10. Effects of flexitime on the organization: the experiences of 196 users in the U.S., 1977.

Nature of Effects	Changes Caused by Flexitime		
	Better	No Change	Worse
	(percent of all users)		
Effects on workers			
Employee morale	97	3	0
Employee commuting	77	18	5
Effects on job performance			
Productivity	48	48	4
Turnover	53	46	1
Absenteeism	73	25	2
Tardiness	84	12	4
Effects on communication			
Internal communication	6	56	38
External communication	14	65	21
Effects on some management aspects			
Coverage of work situations	30	32	38
Employee scheduling	27	35	38
Work scheduling	21	44	35
Difficulty of management job	5	45	50
Effects on costs			
Unit labor costs of production	21	73	6
Overtime costs	44	54	2
Personnel administration costs	5	82	13
Recruiting	65	34	1
Training	5	90	5
Utilities costs	4	70	26
Support services costs (security, cafeteria, etc.)	2	80	18
Effects on customers, suppliers, and the public			
Relationships with customers	22	70	8
Relationships with suppliers	5	91	4
Public relations	43	54	3

Businesspeople explain why productivity goes up under flexitime:

- "It makes individuals of employees, and thereby (gives) more motivation to do better work." (*from a medium-sized wholesaling company in the Northeast*)
- "Allows an employee the option of working when he/she functions best and is most productive." (*from a large insurance company in the Midwest*)
- "(Flexitime) makes employees aware of their responsibility to other workers in attendance and productivity." (*from a small*

industrial manufacturing company in the East)

Of course, there are exceptions—a few cases of adverse productivity effects surfaced. For example, a respondent from a large midwestern insurance company reported, "We suffered some production loss. Certain employees took advantage of their supervisor's not being present when they started work." And sometimes employers are not certain whether flexitime alone led to improved productivity, or whether other factors also had an impact.

Effects on communication. Under a flexitime

system, not all employees are required to be on the job at the same time—an aspect that has created concern about communication problems. The evidence is that in a significant number of instances, communication—especially internal communication—is worsened. (Examples of improved communication are infrequent.) For example, a respondent from a small industrial manufacturing company in the Mid-Atlantic region said, "The man with the answer I need *now* either won't be here for another hour, or he just went home." And a respondent from a large insurance company in the East noted that "Most people choose the earlier times to arrive/leave—thus a skeleton crew remains (and) communications are hampered or may have to wait till the next day." In the majority of cases, however, there are no problems. Among flexitime users, 38 percent reported worsened internal communications. A smaller number—21 percent—reported worsened external communication. Much larger numbers—56 and 65 percent of the users, respectively—reported no change in internal and external communication. In cases where flexitime improved external communication (one out of seven), the causative factor may be that business was being conducted across time zones, which flexitime can obviously facilitate with some workers coming in early and others staying late.

Effects on management aspects. Overall, flexitime is quite likely to increase the difficulty of the management job. Some businesspeople report that flexitime is hard to monitor and easy for employees to take advantage of, and that lack of supervision could be a problem—"not so much that we don't trust employees, but decisions might have to wait for a supervisor to be on hand and production might be held up" (from a medium-sized industrial manufacturing firm in the Midwest). Some supervisors report that their jobs are made harder from the control standpoint. They may perceive a loss of control, and must depend on employees' willingness to cooperate.

But flexitime has favorable as well as unfavorable effects on management tasks. For example, "Supervisors are relieved of the onerous task of monitoring arrival and departure times of their subordinates," according to a utility employing

500 to 1,000 people on the West Coast. And since flexitime provides freedom with individual responsibility, "it leads to better. . .experience with participative approaches to management" (from a medium-sized industrial manufacturing firm on the West Coast).

Flexitime has mixed effects on the personnel coverage of work situations. Worse coverage (caused 38 percent of the time by either the late arrival of some workers or the early departure of others) was experienced somewhat more often than was better coverage (caused 30 percent of the time by the reverse situation—the *early* arrival of some workers or the *late* departure of others). Sometimes crosstraining of employees in back-up services can overcome coverage problems. Similarly, although both employee scheduling and work scheduling were complicated by flexitime in a third or more of the organizations, easier scheduling was also reported in roughly a quarter of them.

Thus it is clear that the flexibility in workers' time schedules under a flexitime system can work to either the advantage or the disadvantage of the employer. Which of these is actually experienced depends, of course, on the specifics of the work setting and on management's skill in responding to the challenge (a potential coverage problem, for example, may be avoided by establishing minimum staffing requirements during periods of flexible hours).

Effects on costs. Flexitime's effects on business costs are negligible. Of the organizations using flexitime, 80 percent or more report no change in personnel administration costs, training costs, or even support services costs (those involving, for example, security or the cafeteria).

Utilities costs, which have been a concern to organizations considering flexitime, remained the same for 70 percent of the users and increased for only 26 percent of them. Increases obviously might occur if the office or plant is open for longer hours to accommodate early-arriving or late-departing flexitime workers.

On the other hand, unit labor costs of production decreased for 21 percent of user organizations, but they remained the same for the largest number of users (73 percent). Thus increased labor productivity (experienced by 48 percent of the users) is not always translated into reduced labor costs.

Flexitime does, however, frequently reduce two cost elements: recruiting and overtime. Recruiting efforts are enhanced by two flexitime effects—reduced turnover and heightened job appeal. Businesspeople explain the recruiting advantage in several ways:

- "(Flexitime) allows fuller utilization of females (who have) skills and abilities, but (who are) unable to work a regular day or evening shift because of family commitments." (*from a large consumer manufacturing firm in the Midwest*)
- "Many top women have family responsibilities—(and are) available only certain hours. If you can fit your hours to their schedule, you get top people and don't have to fool with dunderheads." (*from a small retail trade organization in the Midwest*)
- "We have had new employees take our job, rather than another offer, because of flexitime. Also (it has) held, the grapevine tells us, some who would have left." (*from a small publishing company in the East*)

Overtime reductions, experienced by 44 percent of the users, may stem from the increased labor productivity already noted. Since most flexitime systems used still require an eight-hour workday, employers are obviously not using flexitime as a way of avoiding overtime—by suggesting, for example, that workers voluntarily change their daily hours to accommodate their employer's needs.

Effects on customers, suppliers, and the public. Flexitime frequently improves public relations, seldom affects relationships with suppliers, and only infrequently affects relationships with customers. Opportunities for better customer service (stemming from longer business hours under flexitime) occurred for 22 percent of the flexitime users; worse customer service (resulting, for example, from lack of coverage at certain times) was experienced by only 8 percent of the users.

The Measurement of Flexitime Effects: Is It Data-Based?

How do managers know about the effects of flexitime on their organizations. Do they rely simply on management observation or is their knowledge based on data collected from, say, in-house surveys or analysis of personnel records? (Of course, some of the effects of flexitime—such as, for example, personnel coverage, communication, scheduling, and public relations—are not readily measurable in any rigorous or quantitative way. Respondents were therefore not asked if these experiences were data-based.)

A data basis for measuring flexitime effects was most frequently available for the effects on employees and on job performance. (See Exhibit 11.) For example, 67 percent of employers' experiences with absenteeism and 63 percent of the experiences with employee morale were data-based. Other effects sometimes measured are turnover and productivity—for which, respectively, 46 percent and 44 percent of all users collect data. Obviously, then, the most favorable flexitime experiences reported by employers are frequently data-based and thus documented; they are not just casual impressions.

The availability or lack of data on flexitime effects depends, of course, on the ease and cost of collecting the particular data involved. But their availability also reflects management priorities—thus confirming the importance of flexitime primarily for workers, with secondary job-performance benefits for management. In this light, it is clear that organizations are keenly aware of the challenges to management posed by flexitime, since 40 percent of the flexitime users report that they collect data on the difficulty of the management job (thus this chief negative effect of flexitime is also documented). On the other hand, most of the direct costs of flexitime are not measured—most notably the costs of utilities and labor. Only 19 percent and 10 percent of the users, respectively, collect such data—even though it would not be hard to do so.

Looking Behind Flexitime Experiences: When Are They Good or Bad?

Flexitime is used more frequently in some industries and work technologies than others. Are employers' experiences better in those industries? Some people have expressed concern that flexi-

Exhibit 11. Measurement of flexitime effects.

Effect	Percent of Users Who Collected Data
Effects that are often measured by data	
Absenteeism	67
Employee morale	63
Tardiness	62
Employee commuting	51
Effects that are sometimes measured by data	
Turnover	46
Productivity	44
Overtime Costs	42
Difficulty of management job	40
Effects that are seldom measured by data	
Relationships with customers	23
Utilities costs	19
Personnel administration costs	16
Relationship with suppliers	12
Support services costs	10
Unit labor costs of production	10
Training costs	9

Note: Sample size was different for each effect, with n ranging from 150 to 174.

time may be less successful in small organizations than in large ones. Are the experiences of small users of flexitime in fact less positive than those of large users? Several different flexitime models—with varying degrees of flexibility— are in use. Does one model give better results than another?

In this section, the overall effects of flexitime on the organization are analyzed. Key experiences are reported for individual industries, work technologies, firm sizes, and flexitime models. By comparing these experiences across groups, we can suggest where flexitime is most likely to be successful and why certain effects turn out to be good while others do not. (See Exhibit 12.) The key effects to be analyzed are employee

Exhibit 12. Good and bad effects of flexitime found among 196 users.[a]

Good Effects[b]	Bad Effects[c]	Sometimes Good, Sometimes Bad[d]
Raises employee morale	Management job made more difficult	Coverage of work situations
Reduces tardiness	Internal communication worsened	Employee scheduling
Eases employee commuting		
Reduces absenteeism		
Makes recruiting easier		
Reduces turnover		
Increases productivity		

Notes:
[a] In order from strongest to weakest.
[b] Half or more of all users reported better results here, with few or no worse results reported.
[c] Up to half of all users reported worse results here, with few or no better results reported.
[d] Responses about equally divided here between better, no change, or worse results caused by flexitime.

Exhibit 13. The effects of industry on flexitime experiences.

Percent Reporting

		Better	No Change	Worse

Experience · Industry

There is little or no difference among key industries in:

employee morale
Industry	Better	No Change	Worse
manufacturing	95		5
finance/insurance	98		2
government	97		3

absenteeism
Industry	Better	No Change	Worse
manufacturing	76	22	3
finance/insurance	68	32	
government	73	27	

difficulty of management job
Industry	Better	No Change	Worse
manufacturing	6	37	57
finance/insurance	7	43	50
government	4	39	57

coverage of work situations
Industry	Better	No Change	Worse
manufacturing	30	30	39
finance/insurance	23	43	34
government	41	28	31

Firms in the manufacturing industry experienced worsened communications more often than other firms:

internal communication
Industry	Better	No Change	Worse
manufacturing	3	41	56
finance/insurance	8	69	23
government	10	66	24

external communication
Industry	Better	No Change	Worse
manufacturing	12	55	33
finance/insurance	13	81	6
government	21	58	21

But firms in the manufacturing industry also reported productivity gains and labor cost reductions more often and employee scheduling problems less often than other firms:

productivity
Industry	Better	No Change	Worse
manufacturing	57	36	7
finance/insurance	32	64	4
government	53	43	3

22

Exhibit 13. (continued).

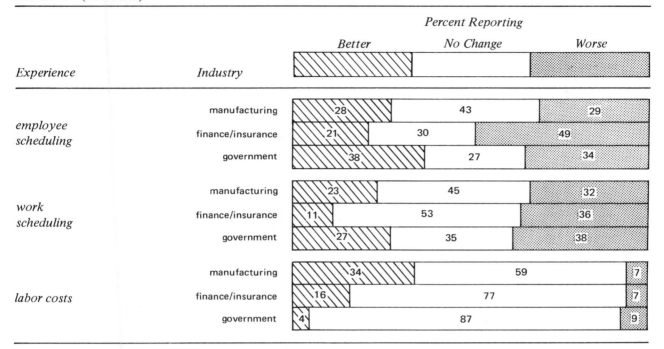

Experience	Industry	Percent Reporting Better	No Change	Worse
employee scheduling	manufacturing	28	43	29
	finance/insurance	21	30	49
	government	38	27	34
work scheduling	manufacturing	23	45	32
	finance/insurance	11	53	36
	government	27	35	38
labor costs	manufacturing	34	59	7
	finance/insurance	16	77	7
	government	4	87	9

Notes: The sample sizes are n=67 for manufacturing, n=48 for finance and insurance, and n=30 for government. The relationship between industry and flexitime effects was tested for statistical significance using the Chi-square statistic. Conclusions in the chart above and the accompanying text adhere to these tests. Because of the small sample size for the government industry, it was excluded from the statistical test; results for the government industry are presented for descriptive purposes only and cannot be considered either significantly better or worse than those of other industries. For some of the contingency tables, a frequency count of less than 5 in a cell required a collapsing of categories; for example, the industry-productivity relationship was tested for two effects, *better* and *not better* (the sum of *no change* and *worse*) because of infrequent *worse* responses. (Even though tests were made in this way, we have not collapsed the *no change* and *worse* categories in the above table.)

morale (the most universal good effect): productivity and absenteeism (two key job-performance measures that often improve under flexitime); internal communication, external communication, and coverage of work situations (three occasional trouble spots for flexitime); difficulty of the management job (the most frequent negative aspect of flexitime); and labor costs.

Industry

For the most part, flexitime experiences do not differ from one industry to another. (See Exhibit 13.) And when they do differ, one industry is no more likely to have good experiences than another. Even though manufacturing firms have the lowest flexitime usage rate, for example, they do not have more bad experiences than do firms in the finance and insurance industry (where flexitime is used most frequently). As a respondent from a medium-sized industrial

manufacturing firm on the West Coast indicated, "Even with continuous process functions, our program has worked most easily in the manufacturing group." Nor, by the same token, do firms in the finance/insurance industry have more good experiences than manufacturing firms. This does not mean that flexitime can be successfully used anywhere, but it does mean that flexitime *is* used in manufacturing firms with results that are just as good, overall, as those in other firms. (These results cannot be taken to mean, however, that experiences with production workers who are on flexitime will be the same as those reported for manufacturing firms, since it is not known how many flexitime workers in manufacturing firms *are* production workers.)

There are no significant differences from one industry to another in experiences with employee morale, absenteeism, difficulty of the management job, or coverage of work situations.

Exhibit 14. The effects of work technology on flexitime experiences.

		Percent Reporting		
		Better	No Change	Worse
Experience	Work Technology			

Goods producers are more likely to experience increased productivity and reduced labor costs than are services producers, but also more likely to have worsened communication and increased difficulty of the management job.

Experience	Work Technology	Better	No Change	Worse
productivity	goods producers	60	33	6
	services producers	45	52	3
labor costs	goods producers	27	68	5
	services producers	16	78	6
internal communication	goods producers	5	40	56
	services producers	6	67	27
external communication	goods producers	13	56	32
	services producers	15	65	20
difficulty of management job	goods producers	6	40	53
	services producers	4	54	42

Mass production technology is associated with an above-average frequency of worsened communication, but also with an above-average frequency of improved productivity and absenteeism.

Experience	Work Technology	Better	No Change	Worse
internal communication	mass production	7	29	64
	not mass production	6	61	33
external communication	mass production	7	28	64
	not mass production	13	67	20
productivity	mass production	56	41	3
	not mass production	46	49	5
absenteeism	mass production	90	10	
	not mass production	70	28	2

In organizations where each worker's tasks require the presence of other workers, management aspects are complicated, and internal communications are worsened.

Experience	Work Technology	Better	No Change	Worse
coverage	presence required	27	22	51
	presence not required	31	35	33

Exhibit 14. (continued).

		Percent Reporting		
		Better	No Change	Worse
Experience	*Work Technology*			
employee scheduling	presence required	24	29	47
	presence not required	27	37	36
work scheduling	presence required	16	44	40
	presence not required	23	44	33
difficulty of management job	presence required		40	60
	presence not required	6	46	48
internal communication	presence required	2	49	49
	presence not required	7	58	35

Notes: The sample sizes are n=63 for goods producers, n=97 for services producers, n=29 for mass production, n=167 for non-mass production, n=45 for presence required, and n=151 for presence not required. The relationships between work technology and flexitime effects were tested for statistical significance using the Chi-square statistic. See notes to Exhibit 13.

Communication, however, is one occasional problem area in the use of flexitime that occurs more frequently among manufacturing users than among those in other industries. For example, 56 percent of all manufacturing users report that flexitime worsens internal communication, while only 23 percent of all finance and insurance users report this problem. A similar difference occurs in its effect on external communication.

On the other hand, manufacturing users have better effects in other areas. They report productivity gains more often than do some other flexitime users (57 percent of the time compared with 32 percent for finance and insurance users). Correspondingly, they report labor cost savings more often, and they report employee scheduling problems less often.

Work Technology

In general, experiences with flexitime are not heavily dependent on an organization's work technology. (See Exhibit 14.) Only a few of the technologies that characterize the work done in an organization affect some of the experiences with flexitime. These work technologies are (1) whether the organization is predominantly a goods producer or a services producer, (2) whether there is mass production using assembly lines or not, and (3) whether each worker's tasks require the presence of other workers or not. (Since the work technologies are characteristic of a substantial number of employees but cannot be identified exactly with *flexitime* employees, their effects may be stronger in some individual cases than suggested here. Results reported here indicate overall tendencies for experiences with flexitime to be either better or worse, depending on the kind of organization using it.)

Producers of goods report improved productivity stemming from flexitime (60 percent of the cases) more often than services producers do (45 percent of the cases). They also report reduced labor costs more often (27 percent versus 16 percent). On the other hand, as Exhibit 14 shows, goods producers are more likely to experience worsened internal and external communication and perhaps increased difficulty of the management job. These differences are similar to those found in manufacturing users versus finance and insurance users of flexitime. For the manufacturing, goods-producing employer, therefore, the use of flexitime brings both positive benefits and management challenges.

Users with technologies involving mass production or assembly-line work report an above-average incidence of worsened internal and external communication caused by flexitime. Nearly two-thirds of the mass-production users report such experiences, whereas only a third or less of the other users report them. By contrast, absenteeism is nearly always improved among mass-production users of flexitime (90 percent of them), but less often improved among other users (70 percent). Similarly, productivity is more often improved.

In organizations where one worker's tasks usually require the presence of other workers, management faces several difficulties under flexitime. Adequate coverage of work situations is one and increased difficulty with the overall management job is another. Coverage, for example, is worse for just over half the users with this technology, compared with only a third of the users without it. In addition, internal communication experiences are more often worsened, as they are in mass-production technologies. Employee scheduling and work scheduling may also worsen, though the differences between industries is not statistically significant.

In sum, it appears that a substantial number of flexitime users with mass-production technologies or where one worker's tasks require the presence of other workers (as are often found in goods-producing firms and in the manufacturing industry) experience some problems with communication (especially internal) and management tasks. On the credit side, however, their good experiences in such job-performance aspects as productivity and absenteeism, and in reduced labor costs, may offset these problems. Other work technologies do not seem to affect the experiences of flexitime users.

The problem of increased management complexity posed by flexitime—involving problems of coverage and scheduling—also has another side: Skillful managers may find ways to decrease management responsibilities in other areas, such as timekeeping and direct supervision. Although difficulties *can* arise when first-line supervisors are not prepared to give up old roles and handle new ones, flexitime can shift some scheduling responsibilities to the workers themselves, thereby releasing supervisors' time for planning, coordinating, and facilitating.

Size of the Organization

There has been concern that flexitime is less suitable for small organizations than large ones. Although this sample does not have enough very small organizations—fewer than 100 employees (n=14)—to report experiences for them separately, there is no evidence that large size confers any advantages. In fact, if there is any difference at all, it is in the favor of smaller organizations (100 to 499 employees), as Exhibit 15 shows. In comparison with larger flexitime users (500 to 1,000 employees), they have a higher frequency of good experiences with productivity and labor costs and a lower frequency of bad experiences with internal communication, coverage, and employee scheduling. In this report, however, the overall relationship between size and experiences is not statistically significant. Perhaps in relatively small organizations where workers know one another, there is an informal system of adjusting work schedules to individual needs that overcomes potential scheduling or coverage problems. In other respects, size is of no consequence. Although these results may spring from other factors associated with size, they do indicate that small size alone should not keep an organization from using flexitime. Rather, the lower usage rate of flexitime among small firms might be explained by information gaps.

Flexitime Model

Does the particular type of flexitime system used by an organization alter the results obtained? Does one flexitime model yield better experiences than another? Two key differences in flexitime models are (1) whether or not employees need to give advance notice before changing their schedules and (2) whether there is one core period or two, including a flexible lunch break. This study reveals no evidence that either model of schedule change or of core time is superior to the other. In particular, the more flexible model (requiring no advance notice and/

Exhibit 15. The effects of size of the organization on flexitime experiences.

Experience	Size of Organization (number of employees)	Percent Reporting		
		Better	No Change	Worse

Small organizations more frequently report better experiences than medium-sized organizations in:

		Better	No Change	Worse
productivity	100–499	56	39	5
	500–1000	34	59	6
	>1000	44	52	4
labor costs	100–499	31	64	6
	500–1000	20	70	10
	>1000	13	82	4
internal communication	100–499	10	61	29
	500–1000	6	45	48
	>1000	6	57	37
coverage	100–499	32	39	29
	500–1000	29	23	48
	>1000	28	34	38
employee scheduling	100–499	37	32	32
	500–1000	23	32	45
	>1000	27	36	37

Notes: The sample sizes are n=41 for 100 to 499 employees, n=36 for 500 to 1000 employees, and n=107 for 1000 employees. The relationships between size and flexitime effects were tested for statistical significance using the Chi-square statistic. See notes to Exhibit 13.

or with two core periods) does not result in any greater frequency of worsened communications, coverage, employee or work scheduling, or difficulty of the management job. Nor, on the other hand, does it yield any greater frequencies of favorable experiences. Thus the choice of flexitime model need not be constrained by concern about either unusually bad or good experiences that it will produce.

Expectations of Non-Users

It is to be expected that the experiences of flexitime users would on balance be favorable—otherwise they would not persist in its use. But what about employers who do not use flexitime? Do they have generally unfavorable expectations of the effects of flexitime? Do they see some potentially good experiences?

In general, employers who do not use flexitime are predictably less optimistic overall about its effects on the organization than actual user experiences would warrant. While both users and non-users agree on the good effects (they identify the same ones), non-users expect more bad effects than users actually experience—and these outweigh the good effects expected. Like users of flexitime, non-users expect flexitime to have

Exhibit 16. Flexitime effects expected by 374 non-users.

| Nature of Effects | Expected Changes Caused by Flexitime | | |
| | Better | No Change | Worse |
	(percent of non-users)		
Effects on Workers			
Employee morale	88	8	4
Employee commuting	55	23	22
Effects on job performance			
Productivity	33	36	31
Turnover	65	30	5
Absenteeism	70	23	7
Tardiness	68	18	14
Effects on communication			
Internal communication	2	26	72
External communication	6	44	50
Effects on some management aspects			
Coverage of work situations	8	11	81
Employee scheduling	6	8	86
Work scheduling	4	12	84
Difficulty of management job	1	11	88
Effects on costs			
Unit labor costs of production	17	47	36
Overtime costs	30	52	18
Personnel administration costs	4	40	56
Recruiting	72	22	6
Training	6	60	34
Utilities costs	2	41	57
Support services costs (security, cafeteria, and so forth)	3	49	48
Effects on customers, suppliers, and the public			
Relationships with customers	6	46	48
Relationships with suppliers	2	71	27
Public relations	39	46	15

overwhelmingly positive effects on morale, commuting, turnover, absenteeism, and tardiness. Unlike users, non-users have mixed expectations concerning the effects on productivity. (See Exhibits 16 and 17.)

Another difference between users and non-users lies in the fear non-users have about flexitime's negative effects on communication, management aspects, and some costs. Many users, for example, report that under flexitime the management job is made more difficult, and a substantial minority also report that internal communication is worsened; non-users are more likely to expect these bad effects and also to expect worsened employee scheduling, work scheduling, and coverage in most cases. And, contrary to the experiences of users, non-users also expect several costs—utilities, personnel administration, and support services—to increase under flexitime.

Differences between user experiences and non-user expectations may result from differences in the particular industry, work technology, or size involved or simply from misperception. The main explanation in this case appears to be the latter.

It is true that communication and some management aspects—especially the overall difficulty

Exhibit 17. Expected good and bad effects of flexitime among non-users.[a]

Good Effects[b]	Bad Effects[c]	Sometimes Good, Sometimes Bad[d]
Raises employee morale	Management job harder	Productivity
Makes recruting easier	Employee scheduling harder	
Reduces absenteeism	Work scheduling harder	
Reduces tardiness	Coverage worse	
Reduces turnover	Internal communication worse	
Eases employee commuting	Utilities costs higher	
	Personnel administration harder	
	External communications worse	
	Support services cost more	
	Relationships with customers worse	

Notes:
[a]In order from strongest to weakest.

[b]Half or more of all non-users expected better results due to flexitime, with few or no worse results expected.

[c]Half or more of all non-users expected worse results due to flexitime, with few or no better results expected.

[d]Responses about equally divided among better, no change, or worse results expected under flexitime.

of the management job and coverage of work situations—are more often problems for users in the manufacturing industry—users who are goods producers, who have mass-production technology, or who have a set-up in which one worker's tasks require the presence of other workers. And because non-users among the research sample are more heavily represented in these areas (59 percent of them are in manufacturing compared with 36 percent of users), they would experience these problems more frequently if they were to be flexitime users. However, flexitime users who *were* in these industry or technology areas did not have bad experiences so often as the non-users overall expected. Furthermore, the other unfavorable effects expected by non-users either do not vary by industry or technology, or they prove, in the experiences of users, to be better in manufacturing and mass-production situations (productivity is an example).

In general, then, it appears that organizations not now using flexitime could do so and obtain favorable overall results—just as present users do. Since the spread of flexitime does not seem to be constrained by lack of opportunities among non-users, the task ahead is one of disseminating information—with the prospect of a substantial payoff from that effort.

4

Long-Term Effects
of Flexitime

The effects of flexitime on the organization using it are favorable overall: improved employee morale, reduced tardiness, easier employee commuting, less absenteeism, easier recruiting, less turnover, and increased productivity—to recapitulate the leading good effects. But do these good effects last? Do long-term users report good results as often as new users do? Or do the good results diminish with the passage of time? Could the good results spring in part from a kind of Hawthorne effect—destined to fade out sometime after flexitime is implemented and becomes routine?

And what about the few drawbacks of flexitime that are occasionally experienced—increased difficulty of the management job, worsened internal communication, and coverage and scheduling problems? Are these problems resolved with longer flexitime experience? Do they diminish with the passage of time?

A number of flexitime models with varying degrees of employee flexibility are in use. What are the trends in the design of flexitime systems? Are they becoming more flexible?

In this section, answers to these questions are suggested by comparing the experiences of long-term with short-term users, by asking users whether they believe their own results from flexitime have gotten better or worse over time, by comparing selected findings from Martin's 1974 survey with comparable data from the pre-

sent survey, and by longitudinally comparing the experiences of a subset of the flexitime users in 1974 with their experiences in 1977. (Of course, these experiences could have been affected by changes over time in a variety of variables other than duration of flexitime usage. In addition, users' responses in some cases are educated guesses and not data-based.)

Do the Good Experiences Last?

The favorable effects of flexitime remain favorable in the long run; they are not transitory. (See Exhibit 18.) Just as many (if not more) long-term flexitime users as short-term users report improved employee relations and job performance. Most employers believe that the good effects of flexitime have remained stable over time—or that they have actually gotten stronger, not weaker. The good effects of flexitime were reported just as frequently in 1977 as they were in 1974 when the average duration of use was much shorter.

In particular, there is not a significant difference in the relative number of long-term versus short-term flexitime users who report better, worse, or unchanged experiences with the usual good effects of flexitime—whether employee morale, commuting, productivity, absenteeism, tardiness, or recruiting. Not even the public relations advantage wears off. The only exception

Exhibit 18. Key effects of flexitime for long-term vs. short-term users (percent reporting each effect).

	Changes Caused by Flexitime					
	Short-Term Users			Long-Term Users		
	Better	*No Change*	*Worse*	*Better*	*No Change*	*Worse*
Usual or Frequent Good Effects						
Employee morale	100	0	0	97	3	0
Employee commuting	77	20	3	77	15	8
Productivity	45	52	3	51	44	5
Turnover	39	61	0	64	36	0
Absenteeism	77	19	4	66	33	1
Tardiness	77	16	7	81	15	5
Recruiting	50	50	0	62	37	1
Overtime	40	60	0	38	60	2
Public relations	37	63	0	46	52	2
Occasional Problems						
Coverage of work situations	43	30	27	36	34	30
Employee scheduling	37	30	33	30	33	37
Work scheduling	30	33	37	25	41	34
Difficulty of management job	0	50	50	5	46	49
Internal communications	3	70	27	8	53	39
External communications	20	67	13	18	56	26

Notes: Short-term means less than one year (n=31); *long-term* means more than three years (n=61).

to this rule is turnover, in which case a substantial number of "no change" reports from short-term users (less than a year's experience with flexitime) are converted to "better" reports among long-term users (those with more than three years' experience). This change is to be expected, since the reduced turnover resulting from flexitime could be realized only after some time had elapsed.

These results are supported by comparing the experiences of these 1977 flexitime users with those of a 1974 sample (from Martin, 1975), some of whom are also represented in the 1977 sample. (See Exhibit 19.) Although not strictly a longitudinal analysis, the two samples are similar except for duration of flexitime use. The average duration of flexitime use in the 1974 sample was one year and four months, while in the 1977 sample it was two years and four months. The longer-duration 1977 users had about the same experiences in job performance changes stemming from flexitime as did the shorter-duration 1974 users. (See Exhibit 20.)

Further evidence of the durability of positive flexitime effects was revealed when 1974 and 1977 responses from a subsample of 21 organizations that were included in both surveys were compared longitudinally on a case-by-case basis.* For example, all 21 organizations reported decreased tardiness in both 1974 and 1977, and 15 of these said that the improvement reported earlier had grown even better over time. Similarly, while only 12 organizations reported lower absenteeism in 1974, the number had increased to 17 by 1977—and no organization felt that absenteeism had grown worse. Lower turnover had been experienced by only 7 respondents in 1974, but by 1977 the number was 11; only the bank that had curtailed use of flexitime felt that early improvements had not lasted. (Of course, a persistently high unemployment rate since 1974

*Included in this common sample are four manufacturers, two transportation firms, eight finance or insurance firms, five government agencies, and two others. In all cases, the majority of employees who were on flexible hours were office workers, though two manufacturers also used the system for plant workers. One bank had curtailed use of flexitime during the 1974-77 interim, one government agency had discontinued use, and the remainder of the organizations continued to use the system for as many (or more) employees as they had previously.

Exhibit 19. Characteristics of the 1974 Martin sample of flexitime users compared with the 1977 Nollen and Martin sample.

Characteristic	1974 Sample (percent)	1977 Sample (percent)
Industry		
Manufacturing	21	36
Transportation, communications, utilities	9	9
Wholesale and retail trade	0	5
Finance, insurance, real estate	31	25
Services	25	9
Government	14	16
Sector		
Private	78	81
profit	67	74
non-profit	11	7
Public	22	19
Number of employees		
Fewer than 100	19	7
100 to 499	21	21
500 to 1,000	13	16
More than 1,000	48	56
Duration of use		
Less than 6 months	18	8
6 months to 1 year	15	11
1 to 2 years	51	26
2 to 3 years	13	20
More than 3 years	3	35
Average duration of use	1.3 years	2.3 years

Note: Sample sizes are n=55 for 1974, n=196 for 1977.

would also result in reduced turnover.) Easier commuting was reported by 18 users in 1974 and again in 1977. A substantially larger number of organizations were basing their responses on quantitative data in 1977 than had done so in 1974.

Productivity was the only flexitime effect reported in which an initial gain had fallen back to its former level. Two organizations had this experience, and in both cases the reports were guesses, not data-based evaluations.

When organizations were asked to give the most important advantage of flexitime, subsample organizations in both 1974 and 1977 (like the larger sample) named improved morale. They wrote, for example, in terms of "gives employees the opportunity to coordinate work and personal responsibilities," "increased autonomy," "greater job satisfaction," "treats em-

ployees as adults," "creates a climate of trust," and "more equity between professionals and nonprofessionals."

Do the Problems Disappear?

The occasional problems raised by flexitime do not seem to disappear with longer use of the system. In comparison with short-term users, there is no decline in the frequency with which long-term flexitime users report worse coverage, scheduling, communication, or difficulty of management tasks. They continue to occur one-quarter to one-third of the time—and up to half the time for difficulty of management tasks. When asked what effect the passage of time had on their experiences with flexitime, the only problem a significant number of 1977 users mentioned as growing worse over time was difficulty of the management job—27 percent as opposed

Exhibit 20. Job performance effects of flexitime in 1977 and 1974 (percent of sample of users reporting each effect).

| | Changes Caused by Flexitime | | | | | |
| | 1974 Users | | | 1977 Users | | |
Job Performance Effects	Better	No Change	Worse	Better	No Change	Worse
Productivity	50	50	0	48	48	4
Turnover	20	80	0	53	46	1
Absenteeism	55	45	0	73	25	2
Tardiness	83	17	0	84	12	4

Notes: Sample size for 1974 is 52; sample size for 1977 is 196. Results for 1974 are from Martin (1975) and from special tabulations from that survey. Because the 1974 and 1977 samples do not contain the identical respondents, the results are not strictly a longitudinal comparison. As Exhibit 19 shows, however, the samples are quite similar in industry, sector, and size-of-firm characteristics. The median duration of use in 1974 was 1.4 years, while in 1977 it was 2.4 years.

to 63 percent who felt it remained stable and 10 percent who felt the problem has lessened. The most frequently mentioned problems in Martin's 1974 survey were supervisory resistance and fear of loss of control, work coverage, and supervisory coverage. Subsample comparisons confirm these conclusions. Maintaining department or supervisory coverage and internal communication continued to be the most frequently mentioned disadvantages. These difficulties were viewed not as unsolvable problems, but as situations that increased the complexity of the management job.

In sum, the picture that emerges from an analysis of the long-term versus short-term effects of flexitime is one of stability. Favorable experiences hold up over time; problem areas continue to challenge management in a minority of the organizations. Flexitime is a relatively simple technology whose good effects are immediately realized but are also solid and persist. However, potential difficulties still need attention even among long-term users, especially in view of changing flexitime models.

Trends in Flexitime Models

The kinds of flexitime models used by employers are quite stable over time. Only 29 percent of the flexitime users in this sample had made changes since they first adopted flexitime. The flexitime models used in 1977 are similar to those used in 1974 by the organizations in Martin's sample. But when changes occurred, they were usually toward greater flexibility.

The degree of flexibility that workers have in varying their hours worked was about the same in 1977 as it was in 1974. Just under a third of all users permitted more or less than eight hours to be worked in each day in both years as long as 40 hours were put in for the week; a few more employers permitted banking and borrowing of hours from one week to the next—8 percent in 1977 versus 2 percent in 1974. The balance of users required eight hours of work each day.

There was a slight trend toward greater flexibility in the use of core time. Comparing 1977 with 1974 patterns, the incidence of a single core time decreased from 64 to 49 percent while the use of double core times (with a flexible lunch period) rose from 29 to 39 percent of all flexitime users. There were also a few more users who had no core time requirements—12 percent in 1977 versus 7 percent in 1974.

In a longitudinal comparison among the subsample of 21 flexitime users for whom there are both 1974 and 1977 data, similar results are obtained. Two of the 21 users had changed from single to double core time, and one had dropped core time requirements by 1977. Banking and borrowing of hours within the workweek was permitted by one user in 1977 who had not allowed it in 1974. Two users had changed their 1974 flexitime model to allow daily variations in arrival and departure times in 1977.

5
Managing Flexitime: Implementation, Problems and Solutions, and Failures

Flexitime is widely distributed across different industry and size groups, and both good and bad experiences are found in each group. In some cases, one flexitime user's bad experience is another's good experience—but the successful use of flexitime always poses some challenge to management. Indeed, flexitime is a management innovation with potentially wide-ranging effects on the organization—it can be a catalyst in organizational change and it can affect the quality of working life. A respondent from a university in the Northwest summed it up:

"Flexitime is primarily used (today) for *supervised* employees. . .yet (it) has always been in operation for individuals who are proven to be 'trustworthy,' i.e., professional. For instance, I go to work *after* my kids get to school. No one complains (nor should they) about *my* production rate. The norm is that supervised employees are not 'trustworthy' and therefore need to have formal designations of time. Yet simultaneously, (rules) remove the joys of personal autonomy and personal judgment concerning the job. Flexitime offers some *important* latitudes for employees under direct supervision to make important choices of their own. It may stimulate a new kind of personal relationship between employer and employee that may be needed (for example, "I have to adjust when my secretary's in-laws come to visit").

In this section, attention is focused on the management of flexitime: where it originates, why and how it is implemented, what accompanying schedule and timekeeping changes are made, what role the labor union has, what problems are encountered and how they are solved and, finally, the anatomy of failure—why flexitime didn't work in the few instances in which it was discontinued.

Why Flexitime Is Implemented

The suggestion to try flexitime often originates with top managers themselves. Only personnel or related departments are more frequent sources. The figures: 45 percent of all flexitime users reported that the idea came from a personnel department, while 39 percent claimed top management as the source. It should be noted here that the respondents themselves were either personnel executives or other top managers. Employees were identified as the source of the suggestion by 7 percent of the users, with a variety of other sources constituting the balance.

After the idea for using flexitime crops up, what are the reasons that impel its implementation? Consistent with users' experiences with flexitime, employees' welfare is the most frequently cited reason—40 percent of the users referred to improving employee morale and satisfaction, and 36 percent mentioned reasons associated with increased employee freedom of

Exhibit 21. Why flexitime is used (n=196).

Reason	Percent of Users
To improve employee morale, satisfaction, motivation, attitudes.	40
To increase employee freedom of choice, flexibility; accommodate their other responsibilities; improve the quality of life both on and off the job; provide equity between professional and other employees; comply with employees who wanted it.	36
To reduce absenteeism, personal time off, sick leave, tardiness, long breaks, and turnover.	23
To increase productivity and efficiency; facilitate production scheduling.	16
To improve services to customers; stay open more hours; increase telephone contact across time zones.	6
Other.	14

Note: Total exceeds 100 percent because of multiple responses.

choice. Job-performance advantages to the employer were also cited frequently. About 23 percent of the users mentioned reduced absenteeism, tardiness, or turnover, and 16 percent cited improved productivity or easier scheduling. (See Exhibit 21.)

Managers stress the mutual advantage to both employees and employers and the low cost of adopting flexitime. For example:

- "(Flexitime) provides a useful benefit to employees at little if any additional cost." (*from a medium-sized federal agency in the Southwest*).
- "It seems like a very innovative way to increase employee dignity and satisfaction at no real cost to the company." (*from a large midwestern industrial manufacturing company*)
- "It's one approach to add to the overall quality of work life." (*from a large midwestern manufacturing company*)
- "We originally implemented flexitime to increase productivity by improving employee morale and reducing unproductive time employees previously spent on personal problems and business affairs." (*from a West Coast utility employing 500-1,000 people*)

Stages of Implementation

The list of implementation steps that can be taken once the idea is raised is long and varied—ranging from discussing flexitime plans with other organizations to documenting the quantitative results of a pilot program. The implementation steps can be broken down into a planning phase and an adoption phase. The planning phase includes all fact-finding and opinion-gathering steps as well as identification of internal management responsibilities. The adoption phase includes any operational changes necessitated by flexitime as well as the actual start-up of flexitime and the possible measurement of its results.

The Planning Phase

According to the sample of flexitime users in this study, implementation steps that are usually taken in the planning phase are (1) meetings with managers and supervisors, (2) meetings with employees, and (3) discussions with people in other organizations. It is not surprising that 85 percent of all users take the first step, nor is frequent consultation with employees surprising (61 percent of all users)—since flexitime is principally intended for them. But, in addition, 61 percent of all users also review state and federal labor laws, indicating widespread awareness of their

Exhibit 22. Implementation steps taken by users of flexitime.

Implementation Steps	Percent of All Users
Planning phase	
Held meetings with managers/supervisors	85
Held meetings with employees	67
Discussed plan with other organizations	61
Reviewed state and federal labor laws	61
Organization member attended a seminar or conference	54
Appointed an internal project director	37
Held meetings with union representatives	15
Utilized services of a time equipment sales company	14
Engaged an outside consultant	2
Adoption phase	
Instituted first on trial basis	86
Changed operating schedule	70
Provided for audit of results	39
Established baseline data for formal evaluation of	
—employee attitudes	37
—business results	26
Employees voted on adoption of flexitime	20
Employees cross-trained	11
Work restructured	8

Notes: Sample size is 196. Totals exceed 100 percent because of multiple responses.

effect (sometimes constraining) on flexitime. In more than half the cases, an organization member attended a seminar or conference. However, an internal project director was appointed in scarcely more than a third of the organizations. The consulting services of a company selling time equipment were utilized as often as the equipment is used—14 percent of users—but outside consultants were seldom used, testifying to the basic simplicity of flexitime. Although only 15 percent of the users consulted with labor unions about adopting flexitime, that percentage represents virtually all the cases in which there were union members on flexitime (see Exhibit 22).

The importance of communication with employees was stressed by several users: "We would recommend a good communication program from the start. This will help sell your ideas to your employees and will establish clear rules or guidelines for employees." "Prior study, surveys, and very gradual implementation with employee input is the key. Don't force it on them. It took us two years for all in one plant to participate."

The Adoption Phase

In the adoption phase, flexitime is usually instituted first on a trial basis—this is the single most frequent implementation step, with 86 percent of users reporting it. In a large majority of cases, the organization's operating schedule is changed to accommodate flexitime: 66 percent of the users are open to employees for longer hours, 33 percent are open to customers or to the public for more hours, and about a quarter of those with shiftwork rearranged their shifts (45 percent of the flexitime users in the sample had more than one shift each day). As many as four users out of ten take no other implementation step. Employees usually do not vote on the adoption of flexitime, work is seldom restructured, and measurement and evaluation of results are carried out in one form or another by less than two-fifths of the users.

Timekeeping Systems

There are basically four methods of timekeeping

for employees on flexitime: (1) the honor system, in which employees are simply trusted to work the required number of hours each day or week and to keep track of their own time (although, of course, supervisors or co-workers may keep a more or less watchful eye); (2) time accumulators, which are special electronic devices that display an employee's time worked over the day or week, but do not record arrival or departure times (they are known by such trade or company names as Flextime, Interflex, or Systematics); (3) computer-based systems, which are entered by insertion of the employee's card in a strategically located input terminal (these systems have the capacity to keep complete payroll records, but give a visual display of hours worked only if the system has a direct link to a computer); and (4) traditional manual record-keeping systems such as time sheets or sign-in/sign-out sheets—or standard time clocks, in which case an employee punches in and out.

As Exhibit 23 shows, the most frequently used timekeeping system for exempt employees on flexitime (those for whom overtime need not be paid—see the notes in Exhibit 23) is the honor system, accounting for just over half the organizations. For non-exempt employees (who are usually blue-collar or lower-level white-collar workers), timekeeping methods differ: The honor system is used less frequently—in 29 percent of the organizations—and manual records or traditional time clocks are the most commonly used method, accounting for 58 percent of all organizations.

Flexitime accumulators or computer-based systems are used in 13 percent of the organizations, for both exempt and non-exempt employees. In most organizations, the timekeeping method that was used before flexitime was introduced continues to be used after it is implemented. When flexitime is first introduced, flexitime accumulators (when they are used) appear to take the place of the honor system for exempt employees, and to take the place of both the honor system and traditional manual records or time clocks for non-exempt employees. Once flexitime is implemented and a timekeeping method chosen, there is little change later in the basic method.

The introduction of flexitime accumulators

Exhibit 23. **Flexitime timekeeping systems for exempt and non-exempt employees, over time.**

Employee Category and Time	Honor System (percent)	Flexitime Accumulator or Computer System (percent)	Manual Records, Time Clocks (percent)
Exempt employees (n=144 firms)			
at present time	52	13	35
when flexitime was first introduced	51	14	35
before flexitime	67	n.a.	33
Non-exempt employees (n=184 firms)			
at present time	29	13	58
when flexitime was first introduced	26	13	61
before flexitime	37	n.a.	63

Notes: Exempt and non-exempt refer to coverage under the Fair Labor Standards Act, which requires overtime to be paid for work beyond 40 hours per week; exempt employees are likely to be in white-collar occupations while non-exempt employees are likely to be in blue-collar and lower-level white-collar jobs. The honor system includes some with supervisory checks; see text for description of flexitime accumulators and computer systems; manual records include time sheets and sign-in/sign-out sheets, and time clocks refer to traditional punch-in/punch-out clocks that record arrival and departure times. Sample sizes are less than 196 because not all users have both exempt and non-exempt employees on flexitime, and because some respondents did not answer questions in this connection.

Exhibit 24. Summary of implementation steps that alleviate flexitime problem areas.

Problem Area Alleviated	Implementation Step			
	Appointed internal project director	Held meetings with managers, supervisors	Held meetings with employees	Instituted first on trial basis
Coverage of work situations		x		
Employee scheduling	x	x	x	
Work scheduling	x		x	
Difficulty of management job	x			
Internal communication	x	x		x

requires some care. The admonition of one flexitime project director—to be sure that flexitime takes nothing away from employees—seems especially true for timekeeping. Any method that implies less trust or more control, both of which are contrary to the spirit of flexitime, is likely to sour employee attitudes.

Consider, for example, one government agency where professional employees had an informal flexible hours arrangement, with the honor system used for timekeeping. Then the agency implemented flexitime with an experimental group composed primarily of the professional employees. When flexitime accumulators were installed, the employees saw this change as imposing new control on them without giving them additional freedom in return. Yet management feared that employees would cheat if the timekeeping equipment was not used. The upshot: The agency reverted to a more limited flexitime model in which employees had to arrive and depart at the same time each day.

Other organizations have found that when timekeeping changes go from high-trust systems to mechanical systems perceived as implying lower-trust, the changes work better when all employees—both exempt and non-exempt—are put on the new system. Another company that made no change in its manual timekeeping system when flexitime was first introduced later adopted time accumulators with good results—after flexitime had proven itself. In this case, the time accumulating equipment was seen as a convenience for all rather than as a management control.

Do Implementation Methods Affect Outcomes?

Does the manner in which flexitime is implemented affect its ultimate success? In particular, do key implementation steps reduce the frequency of problems with flexitime?* The answer is, mostly, yes—the main problem areas in flexitime usage are alleviated by one or more implementation steps in the planning phase. (See Exhibits 24 and 25.) In other cases, however, the expected beneficial effects of certain implementation activities do not show up.

In particular, the two leading flexitime problems (increased difficulty of the management job and worsened internal communication) are experienced less often when an internal flexitime project director is appointed—an implementation step that is taken by only 37 percent of the flexitime users. The seemingly obvious alternative, use of an outside consultant, is taken by only 2 percent of users. This step also appears to give better results in both employee scheduling and work scheduling, thus confirming that it is a critical—but frequently overlooked—step in successful flexitime implementation.

Internal communication experiences were also less likely to be worsened when meetings were held with managers and supervisors before conversion. Inexplicably, however, this implementation step did not alleviate the difficulty of the management job. Nevertheless, such meetings

---

*Not all implementation steps can be cross-tabulated with effects of flexitime (1) because of a lack of clear theoretical link between the two variables or (2) because of small sample size.

Exhibit 25. Implementation steps that alleviate flexitime problem areas.

| Problem Area and Implementation Step | Changes Caused by Flexitime | | |
	Better	No Change	Worse
		(percent of respondents)	

Coverage of work situations may be a problem less frequently when meetings are held with managers and supervisors.

Held meetings with managers, supervisors	30	35	36
Did not hold meetings	30	29	42

Employee scheduling is a problem less frequently and an advantage more frequently when meetings are held with employees and with managers and supervisors, and perhaps also when an internal project director is appointed.

Held meetings with employees	33	36	31
Did not hold meetings	18	34	48
Held meetings with managers, supervisors	31	33	36
Did not hold meetings	14	42	46
Appointed an internal project director	34	31	34
Did not appoint a project director	23	37	40

Work scheduling is a problem less frequently and an advantage more frequently when meetings are held with employees and an internal project director is appointed.

Held meetings with employees	25	43	32
Did not hold meetings	15	46	39
Appointed an internal project director	30	44	26
Did not appoint a project director	17	44	39

Difficulty of the management job is increased less often when an internal project director is appointed.

Appointed an internal project director	7	54	39
Did not appoint a project director	4	40	56

Internal communication is a problem less frequently when meetings are held with managers and supervisors, when an internal project director is appointed, and when the program is first instituted on a trial basis.

Held meetings with managers, supervisors	6	61	33
Did not hold meetings	6	43	51
Appointed an internal project director	10	64	26
Did not appoint a project director	5	52	43
Instituted first on trial basis	7	60	34
Did not institute on trial basis	4	45	51

Notes: Sample sizes for each set of responses range from 51 to 146. Differences in experiences by implementation step are statistically significant according to a Chi-square test except for cases where qualifying language is used.

(as well as meetings with employees) were associated with improved results in such other problem areas as employee scheduling and work scheduling. Indeed, scheduling is not generally a problem area when key implementation steps are undertaken—improved results are cited just as often as worsened results in these cases. Thus potential problems with flexitime are susceptible

Flexitime and Collective Bargaining Issues

Labor union positions on flexitime are critical to its wider use and success. Many unions have been reserved toward if not opposed to it, but others have been innovators. Although no single union position exists, we can examine some key features of union attitudes.

The AFL-CIO approves of flexible working hours in principle because of the greater control they give the individual employee over the work environment. It is the union's position, however, that flexibility should be confined to the eight-hour day and that workers should be involved in developing and implementing flexitime programs. (See John L. Zalusky, Research Department AFL-CIO, *Remarks Before the National Conference on Alternative Work Schedules*, Chicago 20-21 March 1977.) Unions on the whole are proceeding cautiously in the area of flexible working hours and only a few contracts involving flexitime have been negotiated. Issues that may arise in the collective bargaining process include:

1. *Schedule setting*. Unions want to include contract language that assures that employees will not be coerced into electing schedules designed to satisfy production rather than personal needs.

2. *Overtime pay*. Currently, many union contracts call for payment at time-and-a-half for hours worked beyond the normal workday (eight or fewer hours as specified by the contract). Under flexitime, will hours worked beyond this limit be compensated at time-and-a-half only when ordered by management, or also when employees voluntarily work longer one day in order to leave earlier another?

3. *Night differentials and weekend premiums*. Some collective bargaining agreements include higher rates of compensation for work performed after a given hour in the evening or on weekends. Employers are unlikely to establish systems that permit employees to choose these hours if such premiums apply.

4. *Productivity gains*. Flexitime often increases productivity because of decreased absenteeism and tardiness, improved morale, or more efficient scheduling. Will employees share in these gains, either through increased leisure or through higher wages?

5. *Paid time off*. In the past, contracts have frequently called for paid time off to vote, keep medical and dental appointments, or attend to other personal business that could not be conducted outside of working hours. Will this privilege continue or will employees be expected to attend to personal business during flexible periods?

6. *Union meetings*. Can union business be conducted during core time when all are present?

7. *Timekeeping*. Many employees object to time clocks—yet flexitime necessitates a timekeeping system that not only informs non-exempt employees of how many more hours they need to work in order to meet contract requirements, but also maintains records sufficient to meet the demands of wage and hour law. Whether conventional time clocks, automatic time-recording devices, or manual systems are used is a matter for negotiation.

8. *Job classification*. In order to give maximum flexibility to individuals and at the same time maintain production or service, it may be necessary for workers on flexible hours to cover for one another. Will they be allowed to work outside their job classifications?

9. *Excluded employees*. Inevitably, the nature of some jobs bars including the people who hold them in a flexible hours program. Do these workers deserve something like a shift differential because their working conditions, relative to those in other parts of the organization, have worsened?

to management intervention and need not actually become realized problems.

The Role of Labor Unions

Although nearly half the organizations in the sample that use flexitime have a labor union, only 17 percent of them have as many as 10 percent of their flexitime employees in labor unions. Only 7 percent of the flexitime users have half or more of their flexitime employees in a union. This does not mean, however, that labor unions

Exhibit 26. Problems encountered in the use of flexitime (n=112).

Problem	Percent of Responses
Management or supervision problems	34
scheduling more difficult, supervisors work longer, have less flexibility	21
supervisory resistance, fear of loss of control	13
Coverage—too few workers at some places at some times	24
Abuse by workers—cheating on time worked, failure to work in absence of supervisor	10
Timekeeping—employees resent timekeeping device or manual recording difficult	
Flexitime model unsuited—core time too short or too long, lunch period too flexible	6
Communication, coordination	5
Excluded employees	3
Carpools disrupted	2
Other	8

oppose flexitime. There was only one report of such opposition—although some other employers may refrain from proposing flexitime because of concern over adverse union reaction. The exclusion of union members, of course, may also be related to the occupations involved. Clerical jobs, whose holders are less often represented by a union, are more often put on a flexible hours basis than are production jobs, whose holders frequently are union members.

On the other hand, there were only a few reports of union bargaining demands for flexitime; it was seldom a negotiating issue. Instead, the labor union role appears in the vast majority of cases to be *no* role at all. Employers usually do not ask for it. When unions are involved, it is usually in a participatory way, but not formally in labor-management negotiations.

Problems and Solutions

By far the most frequent problems encountered by flexitime users are management or supervision problems and work coverage problems. (See Exhibit 26.) Taken together, they account for well over half of all the problems encountered. Other problems that occasionally occur are abuse of flexitime by employees, timekeeping problems, and an ill-suited flexitime model.

A key part of managing flexitime successfully is to solve these problems when they occur. In general, coverage problems are usually worked out by the employees themselves, who agree voluntarily on how minimum staffing requirements can be met—usually by rotating their schedules and covering for each other. Occasionally, some reduction of flexibility is necessary. Solutions to supervisory problems require experimentation and sometimes modification of the flexitime system. Overcoming supervisors' resistance to flexitime requires educating them in a new concept of supervision—one that emphasizes planning rather than controlling. Of course, it takes time to change attitudes. Pilot project demonstrations of the feasibility of flexitime may be required. Communication problems are solved by a combination of (1) experience with who is at work during what hours and (2) modifications of the flexitime system. Timekeeping problems and employee abuses are solved by changing timekeeping methods, relying on peer pressure to curb offenses, or removing guilty employees from the flexitime system.

Examples of these problems and their solutions, in the employers' own words, are given in Exhibit 27.

Flexitime Failures: Who Discontinues It and Why

Like any management innovation, flexitime will not always succeed. Some failures will be traceable to management problems or to misfits be-

Exhibit 27. Examples of flexitime problems and their solutions (actual reports from flexitime users).

Problem	Solution
Management or supervision problems	
First-line supervisors reluctant.	Training/education—"try it, you'll like it."
Role of first-line supervisor.	Reeducation in job.
Scheduling of meetings was made more difficult.	Earlier scheduling; most problems resolved with minor rearrangements of our own attitudes; i.e., willingness to alter inflexible habits we had gotten comfortable with.
Employees who work as a team cannot agree on a work schedule.	Company "business hours" prevail.
Coffee breaks—we had used a set time for each department, but dropped it with flexible hours. First day everyone went to coffee at the same time and we had standing room only.	We did nothing—next day problem went away. Moral: treat people as adults and they'll act as adults.
Departmental scheduling—allowing too many to use flexitime at the same time.	Require at least 1/3 staffing at all times.
Supervisors not having same degree of flexibility, sometimes required to work longer hours to cover entire workday.	Supervisors decide who will come in early and stay late; they then rotate.
Supervisory resistance—they were suspicious, insecure; doubted that employees would produce.	Launch pilot demonstration project, keep circulating testimonials.
Resistance from senior supervisors who felt loss of status and loss of control, and were unable to internalize the "Theory Y" philosophy that must accompany flexitime.	After 10 to 12 months they had adjusted.
Involvement of first-level supervisors in planning phase.	Extensive meetings on work scheduling processes and employee control procedures.
Coverage problems	
Telephone coverage by secretaries.	They established their own rotating schedule so that at least one person was available to cover phones during normal business hours.
Lack of agreement as to start/stop time between interfacing work groups.	Brought groups together, identified problem, and had it solved by agreement.

Exhibit 27 (continued).

Problem	Solution
Small groups unable to cover some positions if flexitime adopted.	Disallowed small groups to participate.
Receptionist does not arrive until 9:00 a.m.	Another employee had to become familiar with telephone answering and receiving visitors.
Staffing switchboard to closing time on Fridays.	Told department employees to solve it; they did.
Coverage of key desks for inside and outside contacts.	Had to ask a few people to reduce their flexitime opportunities.

Communication and coordination problems

Problem	Solution
Coordinating two-shift operations.	Had day and evening shift make recommendations themselves, and if they couldn't solve it we just put people back on regular shift.
Had an immediate shift to an earlier workday, 7:30 a.m. to 3:30 p.m., which cut down on communication with the West Coast.	Met with department heads and employees to discuss problem and work out coverage to 5:00 p.m.
Interaction with other departments still on an 8:00 to 5:00 schedule.	Personnel from other departments had to adjust their thinking and communications to the core period.

Timekeeping problems and employee abuse of flexitime

Problem	Solution
Minor number of abuses.	Individuals involved put on standard hours.
Employees abusing the honor system of timekeeping.	Staff meetings, constructive administration of discipline.
Not observing core hours requirement.	Talked to all employees; closer supervision.
Honor system not reliable.	Time recording devices a must.
Flexitime accumulators too expensive.	Implemented honor system.
Many employees felt no need to keep time records.	We reiterated our instructions and conducted an audit to assure compliance.
Cheating on time cards.	Peer pressure; employee taken off flexitime if necessary. The employees tend to "police" each other because they don't want to lose flexitime for all.

tween flexitime and its intended usage situation. The failure rate, however, is quite low. Only 15 of the survey respondents were former flexitime users who had discontinued its use; there were 13 continuing successful uses of flexitime for every one failure, or a failure rate of 8 percent. Over half the discontinuers had used flexitime less than a year; the largest number (44 percent) had used it 6 months to a year. About 80 percent of those who dropped flexitime did so before two years had elapsed.

What can be learned from these failures? Why did they happen? What are the pressure points that warrant future management attention?

Although the number of flexitime discontinuers is too small to permit valid comparisons with users, there do not appear to be any gross differences in their characteristics—whether of industry, sector, size, work technology, labor union role, female workforce, or operating schedule. No single dimension leads to failure.

Indeed, the organizations themselves that discontinued flexitime gave a variety of reasons for dropping it. Most frequently, supervisory problems were to blame. Sometimes supervision could not be adequately provided, so coverage and scheduling problems resulted. For example:

- "Supervisors felt that additional work and time on their part was required for planning, controlling, and scheduling matters."
- "It was too difficult to implement companywide, and too difficult for our large department to supervise."

- "Difficult to schedule overtime during peak seasons within our particular flexitime parameters."
- "Difficulty in providing full supervisory coverage."
- "Office was not always 100 percent operational. Control was difficult."

In other instances, supervision problems were related to timekeeping and other specific control issues:

- "Without time cards for everyone, it proved difficult to manage."
- "It became a nuisance to keep track of latecomers." "Significant problems in identifying and controlling tardiness."
- "Due to a lack of controls, abuses occurred. Was a supervision problem, not a problem with the concept."

And occasionally the difficulties posed by communication problems led to the discontinuance of flexitime. For example, "At least one hour was lost each day because departments were on different flexitime hours, making intercompany communication difficult."

In conclusion, it is clear that the important issue in adopting flexitime is not *what* is done, but *how* it's done. Successful use of the system depends not on which model is chosen, but on what steps are followed in implementation. Appointment of a project coordinator is a critical step, as is early involvement of supervisors and employees in the planning process.

Appendix A
Nationwide Projection
of Flexitime Usage

In order to estimate how widely flexitime is used in the U.S., a projection was made from survey responses. The accuracy of the projection depends on several factors—including the size of the sample, the representativeness of the sample, and the degree of response bias involved.

For the 100 percent sample on which to base the nationwide projection, we used only the survey responses (495) from our list of customers of the American Management Associations (AMA) from 1975 to 1977 (first half).* Customers were either seminar attendees or purchasers of AMA publications (There were no AMA seminars on flexitime during that time span, so the sample is not biased in favor of flexitime use on that account.) Restrictions on the population were that the customer should be a senior management officer (for example, president, vice-president for human resources, or a personnel director), and that the size of the customer's firm or agency should be greater than 50 employees. These two restrictions were imposed to ensure that knowledgeable people would answer the questionnaire and to avoid idiosyncratic experiences that may characterize very small users of flexitime. Thus, the population by design was

*Additional survey responses were obtained from known or suspected flexitime users to ensure that there would be a large enough number of responses from users on which to base inferences about the effects of flexitime. We did not include these responses from known or suspected users in computing the nationwide usage rate, however, because doing so would have introduced extreme bias and resulted in a distorted (much too high) usage rate.

not representative of all U.S. employers and required adjustments to obtain a nationwide projection.

We needed to make two kinds of adjustments to the AMA customer sample:

1. *An adjustment to correct the sample for its unrepresentative nationwide industrial distribution.* We started by taking the flexitime usage rate for each individual industry in our sample and weighted each of those rates by the national industrial distribution of firms in each corresponding industry. Exhibit 28 shows how the flexitime usage rate of survey respondents in each major industry group was weighted by its share of all employers (corporations) in the U.S. to obtain a nationwide projection of flexitime usage. This figure was computed as the sum of the products of each line of column 2 by its corresponding line in column 3; it gave a value of 16.6 percent.

2. *An adjustment for response bias.* We needed to adjust for response bias because the response rate of the AMA customer list was only 24 percent. The flexitime usage rate among respondents might not be the same as among those who did not respond. Indeed, the resultant bias in a flexitime usage rate based on this response is likely to be upward (that is, too high) because users are more likely to be better motivated to respond to the questionnaire than are non-users. The degree of bias was determined by (1) telephoning 100 randomly selected non-respondents

Exhibit 28. Industrial distribution of survey respondents and all U.S. corporations—showing flexitime usage rate by industry, 1977.

Industry	(1) Survey Respondents[a] (percent)	(2) All U.S. Corporations[b] (percent)	(3) Flexitime Usage Rate[c] (percent of respondents)
Manufacturing (n=266)	56	13	12.4
Transportation, communication, and utilities (n=50)	10	4	16.0
Wholesale and retail trade (n=35)	8	35	17.0
Finance, insurance, and real estate (n=75)	16	26	22.7
Services (n=34)	9	22	11.8
Government (n=5)[d]	1	N.A.	N.A.
All industries (n=465)[e]	100	100	16.6

Notes:

[a]Respondents from AMA customer sample only; sample of known or suspected flexitime users excluded. See the Introduction, page 4.

[b]Because the AMA customer sample was restricted to firms or agencies with more than 50 employees, partnerships and proprietorships are unlikely to be included in the sample (on the assumption that most of them would fall below the size restriction) and hence they are also excluded from the U.S. industrial distribution of firms. The source for the latter is *Statistical Abstract of the U.S.* (Washington, D.C.: U.S. Government Printing Office).

[c]Unadjusted for response bias; see text.

[d]Because the sample size in the government industry is too small to permit a valid measure of flexitime usage in government, and because no comparable data were available to permit knowledge of the share of government organizations in the distribution of all U.S. employers, the government industry is excluded from the nationwide projection of flexitime usage. See, however, page 47.

[e]Here, n=465 rather than 495 since users in some industries were deleted from the analysis because of the small number of responses in those industries.

to the mailed questionnaire in the AMA customer list, (2) determing the flexitime usage rate among these 100, and (3) using the resulting figure to further adjust the flexitime usage rate.

Since the industrial distribution of those telephoned was similar to that of the questionnaire respondents, the flexitime usage rate among the telephoned organizations, which was 11 percent, was used to adjust downward the mail survey usage rate (previously adjusted, as explained earlier, for conformance to the U.S. industrial distribution of employers). The formula was: Industry-adjusted survey usage rate (16.6 percent) multiplied by the ratio of the "true" usage rate (from telephone calls)* to the raw upward-biased (from customer returns) usage rate:

$$16.6 \text{ percent} \times \frac{11.0 \text{ percent}}{14.3 \text{ percent}} = 12.8 \text{ percent}$$

*It is not strictly true because it reflects an industrial distribution of firms that does not match that of the U.S. overall.

The result is the nationwide projected flexitime usage rate of 12.8 percent of all organizations (nongovernment, with more than 50 employees).

The meaning here of the term *organization* is usually the entire company, since 70 percent of the survey responses were for the entire company. In 20 percent of the responses, however, *organization* refers to headquarters, division, or a branch of the entire company. Thus the flexitime usage rate referring strictly to entire companies might slightly exceed 12.8 percent.

The chief remaining source of error, if any, in the nationwide projection of flexitime usage is likely to be in hard-to-measure but salient characteristics of AMA customers that are different from other managers. If, as one example, AMA customers are more innovative or more human resources-oriented than other managers are, and if flexitime is perceived by AMA customers as an innovative and human resources-oriented policy, then the flexitime usage rate estimated from this sample would be too high.

The nationwide projected share of employees who are on flexitime—5.8 percent—was calculated from survey results indicating that, on the average, 45 percent of a user organization's workforce was on flexitime (45 percent × 12.8 percent = 5.8 percent). The number of employees on flexitime nationwide is smaller than the number of organizations that use flexitime because even in user organizations, only *some* of the employees are on flexitime (with other employees remaining on standard or other work schedules). This calculation assumes that the proportion of a user's workforce on flexitime does not vary according to the size of the organization. The figure applies to employees in private sector firms with 50 or more employees, and does not include self-employed workers or those professionals, managers, and salespeople who have long set their own schedules without formally calling the activity flexitime.

The estimate that 2.5 to 3.5 million workers in the U.S. are on flexitime used the 5.8 percent figure (above) and additional assumptions. First, the total number of employed persons in the U.S. (about 88 million in 1977) was reduced by the number of self-employed workers (about 8 million) and by an assumed number—one-half—of salaried professionals, managers, and salespeople who unofficially and informally set their own schedules and thus are not part of a formal flexitime program (perhaps 9 million people). In order to be conservative, we used a lower flexitime usage rate than the survey-determined rate for industries and employees not covered by the survey—government workers, agriculture, mining, and construction industries; and employees in firms with less than 50 employees. However, federal government use of flexitime is estimated to be 200,000 workers, or 7 percent of total federal employment. (The source is Ms. Barbara Fiss of the U.S. Civil Service Commission.) These procedures resulted in an estimated 2.5 to 3.5 million employees on flexitime—with the extremes of the range depending on whether a 1 percent or a 6 percent flexitime usage rate is assumed for employment not covered by the survey, and depending on how many professionals, managers, and salespeople are assumed to be "eligible" (that is, not already using it) for flexitime.

Appendix B
Legislation Relevant to
Alternative Work Schedules

A number of laws are relevant to the use of flexitime and other alternative work schedules—with some laws facilitating and some restricting such use. Here, we'll present and discuss the use of alternative work schedules in connection with (1) equal employment opportunity legislation and (2) labor laws—both current and proposed.

Equal Employment Opportunity Legislation

Some of the groups protected by equal employment opportunity law are the same groups who often have difficulty working full-time, fixed-hour schedules: women, older persons, and the handicapped. Employers may find that alternative work schedules, particularly part-time employment and flexitime, help in reaching affirmative action goals. Recruitment of women is easier when flexible schedules permit those who have home and child-care responsibilities to better coordinate their dual roles. Moreover, advancement of women is facilitated when schedule variability encourages more women to remain on the job and in the career track during childbearing years. Older and handicapped people who find it difficult to use public transportation under crowded rush-hour conditions find it considerably easier to do so in off-peak hours. (And members of either group who find full-time work too physically taxing may prefer part-time

employment.) The relevant laws and regulations are summarized below:

1. *Title VII of the Civil Rights Act of 1964* (as amended by the Equal Employment Opportunity Act of 1972) prohibits discrimination based on race, color, religion, sex, or national origin in any term, condition, or privilege of employment. The Equal Employment Opportunity Act strengthened the powers and expanded the jurisdiction of the Equal Employment Opportunity Commission (EEOC) in enforcement of the law. It now covers:

- All private employers of 15 or more persons.
- All educational institutions, public and private.
- State and local governments.
- Public and private employment agencies.
- Labor unions with 15 or more members.
- Joint labor-management committees for apprenticeship and training.

EEOC receives and investigates job discrimination complaints, and when it finds reasonable cause for justifying the charges, it attempts through conciliation to reach an agreement eliminating all aspects of discrimination revealed by the investigation. If conciliation fails, EEOC goes directly to court to enforce the law. Discrimination charges may be filed not only by aggrieved employees and job applicants, but also by organizations on their behalf.

2. *Executive Order 11246* (as amended by Executive Order 11375), issued by President Johnson in 1965, requires formulation of Affirmative Action Programs by all federal contractors and subcontractors and requires that firms with contracts exceeding $50,000 and 50 or more employees develop and implement written programs, which are monitored by the Office of Federal Contract Compliance of the U.S. Department of Labor. Program requirements include identifying areas of minority and female underutilization, numerical hiring and promotion goals, and other actions to increase minority and female employment in job classifications where they are currently underrepresented.

3. *The Equal Pay Act of 1963* (an amendment to the Fair Labor Standards Act) requires all employers subject to the Fair Labor Standards Act (FLSA) to provide equal pay for men and women performing similar work. The FLSA covers workers in interstate commerce—including executive, administrative, professional, and outside sales personnel and employees of the federal government. Its provisions are enforced by the Wage and Hour Division of the Employment Standards Administration of the U.S. Department of Labor. Complaints can be made by letter, telephone, or in person at the nearest Wage and Hour Division office.

4. *The Education Amendments Act of 1972,* Title IX, which extends coverage of the Equal Pay Act to educational institutions, also prohibits discrimination on the basis of sex against employees or students of any educational institution receiving financial aid. It is enforced by the Office of Civil Rights, U.S. Department of Health, Education and Welfare.

5. *Title VI of the Civil Rights Act of 1964* prohibits discrimination based on race, color, or national origin in all programs or activities that receive federal aid. Employment discrimination is prohibited if a primary purpose of federal assistance is to provide employment—for example, apprenticeship, training, or work-study programs. Sex discrimination is not explicitly barred by Title VI, but various federal agencies have included prohibition of sex discrimination in their own regulations.

6. *The Age Discrimination in Employment Act of 1967* prohibits employers of 25 or more persons from discriminating in any area of employment against people 40-65 years old because of age. It is enforced by the Wage and Hour Division of the U.S. Department of Labor.

7. *The Rehabilitation Act of 1973,* Section 503, prohibits employment discrimination against qualified handicapped people by an employer with a federal contract or subcontract of $2,500 or more.

8. *State and local laws* that prohibit employment discrimination have been enacted in some places. When the Equal Employment Opportunity Commission receives discrimination charges, it defers them for 60 days to agencies with comparable jurisdiction and enforcement sanctions in certain states. If satisfactory remedies are not achieved, charges revert to EEOC for resolution.

Current Labor Law

Several elements of labor law are potential hindrances to the use of alternative work schedules. Some new legislation, on the other hand, encourages their use. The key laws and their effects are as follows:

Overtime Law

1. *The Walsh-Healy Public Contracts Act* (41 U.S.C. 35) sets basic labor standards for employees working on U.S. Government contracts to manufacture or furnish more than $10,000 worth of goods. Its overtime provisions require payment at time-and-a-half for hours worked in excess of forty per week or eight per day. The latter provision may be troublesome for users of flexitime and compressed workweeks.

2. *The Contract Work Hours and Safety Standards Act* (40 U.S.C. 328) applies to U.S. Government construction contracts exceeding $2,000, service contracts exceeding $2,500, and supply contracts exceeding $2,500 but less than $10,000. It, too, specifies payment at time-and-a-half after eight hours per day.

3. The amended *Fair Labor Standards Act* of 1938, as amended by P.L. 93-259, April 18,

1974, covers all employees in interstate commerce and public administration. It requires payment of overtime at time-and-a-half after 40 hours per week. There are some statutory exemptions from overtime, however—for example, farm workers, railroad and airline workers, and interstate truck drivers.

4. *The Federal Pay Act* (U.S. Code, title 5) establishes a basic 40-hour workweek for full-time U.S. Government employees and provides payment at time-and-a-half for hours worked in excess of eight per day. Unless an agency would be seriously handicapped in carrying out its function or costs would be substantially increased, tours of duty must be scheduled not less than one week in advance—and, whenever possible, on five consecutive days of equal length Monday through Friday. Breaks of more than one hour may not be scheduled on a basic workday. These provisions limit the use of flexitime and preclude the use of compressed workweeks.

Equal Treatment in Hours, Pay, and Benefits

1. *The Equal Pay Act of 1963,* an amendment to the Fair Labor Standards Act, prohibits sex-based discrimination in the payment of wages for work that requires equal skill, effort, and responsibility and is performed under similar working conditions. Pay is defined as both remuneration for employment (including overtime) and employer contributions to fringe benefit plans. Thus payment of different wages and fringe benefits to part-time and full-time employees is legal as long as (1) difference in working time is the basis for the differential and (2) the pay practice is applied uniformly to men and women. An example of illegal discrimination would be payment of higher wages to male part-time workers than to female full-time workers for equal work.

2. *The Employee Retirement Income Security Act* of 1974 (P.L. 93-406) requires that persons employed 1,000 or more hours per year (roughly half-time) must be eligible for company-sponsored pension plans.

3. *State protective laws* that limit the number of hours a woman can work per day have been declared sex discriminatory under the provisions of Title VII of the Civil Rights Act of 1964 as amended by the Equal Opportunity Act of 1972. Many states have repealed these laws. Waivers are usually available in those that have not.

4. *Social Security tax* (FICA) must be paid on part-time employees as well as full-time employees. The present rate (fiscal 1978) is 6.05 percent of the first $17,700 earned per annum, payable by both employer and employee. This means that part-time employees entail higher FICA costs for employers if the part-timers replace full-time workers and are paid at a full-time equivalent rate exceeding $17,700. Such cases are infrequent.

5. *Federal unemployment compensation tax* must be paid by employers on both part-time employees and full-time employees. The rate is 3.4 percent of the first $4,200 of annual earnings. This means that if part-time employees replace full-time employees, fringe benefit costs go up—but the dollar amount is small. *State unemployment compensation* laws differ. In Washington, D.C., the employer tax is 2.7 percent of the first $4,200 earned by full-time and part-time employees.

6. *The Emergency Jobs Program Extension Act* (P.L. 94-444)—passed on October 1, 1976, to authorize funds to carry out Title VI of the Comprehensive Employment and Training Act of 1973—stipulates that the household support obligations of eligible applicants for public service jobs be taken into account by prime sponsors, and that special consideration be given to such alternative working arrangements as flexible hours, shared time, and part-time employment, particularly for older people and for parents of young children.

Proposed Federal Legislation

Several bills intended to increase the use of flexible working hours, compressed workweeks, and part-time employment have been introduced in the 95th Congress.

1. *H.R. 7130,* sponsored by Representative William Armstrong (R.-Col.), would amend the Walsh-Healy Act to exempt from overtime premiums those employees who worked four or fewer days in any one week, and ten or fewer hours in any one day. This bill would facilitate

the use of four-day/forty-hour schedules, but leave intact constraints against varying the length of the workday when a five-day flexitime plan is used.

2. *The Flexible and Compressed Work Schedules Act of 1977*, S.517 and H.R. 7814, introduced respectively by Senator Gaylord Nelson (D.-Wis.) and Representative Stephen Solarz (D.-N.Y.), modify section 7 of the Fair Labor Standards Act and titles 5 and 38 of the U.S. Code for three years in order to permit experiments with alternative work schedules for federal employees. These laws currently require overtime premiums when employees work more than forty hours a week or eight hours a day, thus constraining the use of four/forty or other compressed workweeks and use of flexible hours systems that permit employees to vary the length of their workday or carry over debit or credit hours from one week to the next. The legislation would permit full-time employees included in a flexitime program to accumulate not more than ten hours of credit per biweekly period and part-time employees to carry over not more than one-eighth of their biweekly work requirement.

Of course, overtime ordered by management would continue to be paid at time-and-a-half. Those on compressed work schedules would not receive premium pay for regularly scheduled working hours over eight per day, but would be paid at time-and-a-half for any additional hours ordered by management. Participation of agencies in experimental programs would be voluntary. The U.S. Civil Service Commission would approve a limited number of proposals for alternative work schedules and evaluate their outcomes relative to commuter traffic, utilization of mass transit, service to the public, efficiency of government operations, and increased full-time and part-time job opportunities.

3. *The Federal Employees Flexible and Compressed Work Schedules Act of 1977*, H.R. 2732, sponsored by Representative Stephen Solarz (D.-N.Y.), differs from S. 517 and H.R. 2903 in that it would require all federal agencies to experiment with alternative work schedules unless exempted by the U.S. Civil Service Commission.

4. *The Part-Time Career Opportunity Act*, S. 518, H.R. 1627, requires most federal executive agencies to make 10 percent of their positions at all levels through GS-15 available on a part-time basis. There would be a five-year phase-in period, and no full-time position occupied by an employee could be abolished in order to create part-time positions. Part-time employees would be counted against personnel ceilings on the basis of the fractional part of the week they worked and would receive fringe benefits prorated to their hours of work. The only difference between the Senate version introduced by Senator Nelson and the House version introduced by Representative Yvonne Burke (D.-Cal.) is that the former defines part-time as less than 40 hours per week while the latter defines it as 16 to 30 hours per week.

5. *The Private Sector Part-Time Employment Act*, H.R. 2402, is designed to stimulate part-time employment in the private sector and relieve high unemployment among women, youths, older persons, and the handicapped. Sponsored by Representative Barber Conable (R.-N.Y.), it provides a tax credit to employers who add permanent part-time employees to their existing staffs. Part-time employees would have to be given work, payment, and fringe benefits, and promotional opportunity equal to that of full-time employees. However, no full-time worker could be laid off in order to hire part-time workers. To encourage part-time employment in higher level positions, larger tax credits would be given for higher salaries, up to a maximum of 25 percent of earnings. The bill would be in effect for three years after date of passage.

6. *The Human Resources Development Act of 1977*, H.R. 2596, sponsored by Representative Stanley Lundine (D.-N.Y.), is intended "to promote economic stability by increasing productivity, improving job security, encouraging retention of jobs in lieu of cyclical layoffs, and promoting the better use of human resources in employment." Grants and loan guarantees would be awarded to employers who undertook. . ."to improve productivity and quality of working life (through projects including) redesign of tasks, responsibilities, and time patterns connected with particular units of employment." States, units of local government and combinations of such units, institutions of higher education, and private employers (including labor organizations) would be eligible for assistance.

Bibliography

1. Allenspach, Heinz, *Flexible Working Hours* (Geneva: International Labour Office, 1975).

2. Baum, Stephen J., and Young, W. McEwan, *A Practical Guide to Flexible Working Hours* (Park Ridge, N.J.: Noyes Data Corporation, 1974).

3. Best, Fred, and Stern, Barry, "Education, Work and Leisure—Must They Come in That Order?" *Monthly Labor Review,* July 1977.

4. Bureau of National Affairs, "Flexible Working Hours Concept Growing but Unions Take Dim View of Idea," *Daily Labor Report,* February 13, 1974, pp. C1-C6.

5. Bureau of National Affairs, "Flexible Hours Idea Being Applied on Limited Basis in Public Sector," *Daily Labor Report,* May 2, 1974, pp. C1-C5.

6. Bureau of National Affairs, "Flexible Working Schedules Take Hold in Europe, Arouse Mixed Interest Here," *Daily Labor Report,* January 15, 1974, pp. C1-C5.

7. Bureau of National Affairs, *ASPA-BNA Survey: The Changing Workweek* (Washington, D.C.: Bureau of National Affairs, 1972).

8. Davis, Herbert J., and Weaver, K. Mark, *Alternate Workweek Patterns: An Annotated Bibliography of Selected Literature* (Washington, D.C.: National Council for Alternative Work Patterns, in press).

9. Elbing, Alvar O.; Gadon, Herman; and Gordon, John R.M., "Flexible Working Hours: It's About Time," *Harvard Business Review,* January-February 1974, pp. 18-33.

10. Evans, Archibald A., *Flexibility in Working Life* (Paris: Organization for Economic Cooperation and Development, 1975).

11. Jaffe, Abram; Friedman, Nathalie; and Rogers, Theresa, "Rearranged Work Schedules in the Private Sector" (Columbia University, forthcoming).

12. Greiner, John M., "Employee Incentives in Local Government: Repackaging Working Hours," in National Commission on Productivity and Quality of Working Life, *Employee Incentives to Improve State and Local Government Productivity* (Washington, D.C.: U.S. Government Printing Office, 1975, pp. 102-111).

13. Golembiewski, R.T.; Hilles, R.; and Kagno M.S., "A Longitudinal Study of Flexi-Time Effects: Some Consequences of an OD Structural Intervention," *Journal of Applied Behavioral Science* 10 (October-November 1974), pp. 503-532.

14. Haldi Associates, Inc., *Alternative Work Schedules: A Technology Assessment* (Springfield, Va: National Technical Information Service, in press).

15. Hedges, Janice M., "Flexible Work Schedules: Problems and Issues," *Monthly Labor Review,* February 1977.

16. Hopp, Michael, and Sommerstad, C.R., *A Three Year Follow-up of the Flexible Work Hours Program in CDC's Aerospace Operations* (Minneapolis: Control Data Corporation, 1975).

17. Magoon, Warren, and Schnicker, Larry, "Flexible Hours at State Street Bank of Boston: A Case Study," *The Personnel Administrator,* October 1976.

18. Maric, D., *Adapting Work Hours to Modern Needs* (Geneva: International Labour Office, 1977).

19. Martin, Virginia H., *Hours of Work When Workers Can Choose: The Experience of 59 Organizations with Employee-chosen Staggered Hours and Flexitime* (Washington, D.C.: Business and Professional Women's Foundation, 1975).

20. Meyers, Robert, "Workers Banish Time Clock: New System Permits Flexible Starting Hours," *Washington Post,* August 3, 1976, p. A1.

21. National Council for Alternative Work Patterns, *National Directory of Organizations Using Alternative Work Schedules* (Washington, D.C.: National Council for Alternative Work Patterns, in press).

22. Nollen, Stanley D.; Eddy, Brenda B.; and Martin, Virginia H., *Part-Time Employment: The Manager's Perspective* (New York: Praeger Publishers, 1978).

23. O'Malley, Brendan, and Selinger, Carl, "Staggered Work Hours in Manhattan," *Traffic Engineering and Control,* January 1973, pp. 418-427.

24. Owen, John D., "Flexitime: Some Management and Labor Problems of the New Flexible Hour Scheduling Practices," *Industrial and Labor Relations Review,* January 1977, pp. 152-61.

25. Port Authority of New York and New Jersey, Planning & Development Department, *Flexible Work Hours Experiment at the Port Authority of New York and New Jersey* (New York: Port Authority of New York and New Jersey, 1975).

26. Port Authority of New York and New Jersey, *Staggered Work Hours Study,* Final Technical Report, August 1977, prepared for Urban Mass Transportation Administration, Washington, D.C. (National Technical Information Service, Springfield, Virginia, forthcoming).

27. Schein, Virginia E; Maurer, Elizabeth H.; and Novak, Jan F., "Impact of Flexible Working Hours on Productivity," *Journal of Applied Psychology,* August 1977, pp. 463-465.

28. Shenahan, Eileen, "Flexible Hours Found Beneficial," *New York Times,* July 7, 1975, p. C37.

29. Swart, J. Carroll, *A Flexible Approach to Working Hours* (New York: AMACOM (division of American Management Associations), 1978.

30. "The Flexitime Concept Gets a Wider Test," *Business Week,* May 24, 1976, pp. 37-38.

31. U.S. Comptroller General, *Contractors Use of Altered Work Schedules for Their Employees—How Is It Working?* PSAD-76-124 (Washington, D.C.: U.S. Government Accounting Office, April 7, 1976).

32. U.S. Congress. House Committee on Post Office and Civil Service, *Alternative Work Schedules and Part-Time Career Opportunities in the Federal Government, Hearings before the Subcommittee on Manpower and Civil Service on H.R. 6350, H.R. 9043, H.R. 3925, and S. 792,* 94th Cong; 1st sess., 1975.

33. U.S. Congress. House Committee on Post Office and Civil Service, *Part Time Employment and Flexible Work Hours, Hearings before the Subcommittee on Employee Ethics and Utilization on H.R. 1627, H.R. 2732, and H.R. 2930,* 95th Cong; 1st sess., 1977.

34. U.S. Congress. Senate Committee on Labor and Public Welfare, *Changing Patterns of Work in America, 1976. Hearings before the Subcommittee on Employment, Poverty, and Migratory Labor,* 94th Cong; 2d sess., 1976.

35. U.S. Geological Survey, Branch of Management Analysis and Branch of Personnel, *Planning for Implementation of Flexible Working Hours,* Interim Report (Reston, Virginia: U.S. Geological Survey, 1975).

36. Wackett, Ronald, Assistant Director of Fringe Benefits Retail Clerks International Association, remarks before the National Conference on Alternative Work Schedules, Chicago, March 20-22, 1977.

37. Wade, Michael, *Flexible Working Hours in Practice* (New York: Halsted Press, a division of John Wiley & Sons, Inc., 1974).

38. Weinstein, Harrier G., *A Comparison of Three Alternative Work Schedules: Flexible Work Hours, Compact Work Week, and Staggered Work Hours* (Philadelphia: University of Pennsylvania, The Wharton School, Industrial Research Unit, 1975).

39. White, Warren, *Flexitime at the First National Bank of Boston* (Washington, D.C.: National Center for Productivity and Quality of Working Life, Longitudinal Study not yet complete).

40. Young, W. McEwan, "Applying Flexible Working Hours in Production Areas," *The Production Engineer,* April 1976, pp. 187-190.

41. Zagoria, Sam, "Flexitime: A City Employee Pleaser," *Nation's Cities,* February 1974, pp. 42-46.

42. Zaluski, John L., Research Department AFL-CIO, remarks before the National Conference on Alternative Work Schedules, Chicago, March 20-22, 1977.

43. Zawacki, R.A., and Johnson, J.S., "Alternative Workweek Schedules: One Company's Experience with Flexitime" (Hewlett-Packard), *Supervisory Management,* June 1976, pp. 15-19.

5 871